Nursing as a Spiritual Practice

A Contemporary Application of
Florence Nightingale's Views

For Jon Arca
who understands
ms nightingale
Joan Mevaue

Janet Macrae, PhD, RN, is an adjunct faculty member in the Advanced Practice Holistic Nursing Program at New York University, and also maintains a private nursing practice specializing in therapeutic touch. She has taught over 350 Therapeutic Touch workshops nationwide and is the author of *Therapeutic Touch: A Practical Guide* (Alfred Knopf, 1987). She co-edited *Suggestions for Thought* by Florence Nightingale (University of Pennsylvania Press, 1994) and lectures extensively on Nightingale's spiritual philosophy and its significance for modern health care.

Nursing as a Spiritual Practice

A Contemporary Application of
Florence Nightingale's Views

Janet A. Macrae, PhD, RN

 Springer Publishing Company

Springer Publishing Company, Inc.
536 Broadway
New York, NY 10012-3955

Acquisitions Editor: Ruth Chasek
Production Editor: Pamela Lankas
Cover design by Susan Hauley

01 02 03 04 05 / 5 4 3 2 1

Library of Congress Cataloging-in-Publication-Data

Macrae, Janet, 1947–
    Nursing as a spiritual practice : contemporary application of Florence
Nightingale's views / Janet Macrae.
        p. cm.
    Includes bibliographical references and index.
    ISBN 0-8261-1387-7
    1. Nursing—Religious aspects.   2. Nightingale, Florence, 1820–1910.
3. Spiritual life.   I. Title.

RT85.2.M33 2001
610.73—dc21   00-064096

Printed in the United States of America by Sheridan Books, USA

To my parents:

Marian and Edwin Macrae

Contents

Preface

Florence Nightingale was the legendary "lady with the lamp" during the Crimean War (1854–1856). As Superintendent of Nurses for the British Army, her expertise in the field of public health, her administrative genius, and her therapeutic presence have gone down in history. She is considered the founder of modern nursing because, as a pioneer in the use of statistics, she laid the foundation for research-based practice.

What is not widely known, however, is that Nightingale had a profoundly spiritual, as well as scientific, view of nursing practice. She presented her spiritual views in a three-volume, 829-page manuscript entitled *Suggestions for Thought,* which she had privately printed in 1860. She developed her spiritual philosophy early in life and although she lived to the age of 90, she never changed its central principles. The views Nightingale expressed in *Suggestions for Thought* provided the foundation for her lifelong work in nursing, hospital management, and public health. At age 53, she published two articles in *Fraser's Magazine* (1873a, 1873b), which contained some of the ideas developed at length in *Suggestions for Thought.* Her thinking about spiritual matters was very radical for her time, and some readers, shocked by her views, wrote to tell Nightingale that they would pray daily for her conversion (Cook, 1913).

Nightingale's spiritual views are now accessible in an edited version of *Suggestions for Thought* published by the University of Pennsylvania Press (Calabria & Macrae, 1994). The edited version contains an extensive introduction and commentaries that place Nightingale's work in a historical and biographical context. *Nursing as a Spiritual Practice: A Contemporary Application of Florence*

Nightingale's Views provides an in-depth discussion of the significance of Nightingale's spiritual views to nursing practice in the twenty-first century, and much of the text is based on the material in *Suggestions for Thought* (1860/1994).

Chapter 1 explores Nightingale's intellectual background. Rather than a chronological biographical sketch, its focus is the major influences—ideas, persons, and events—that helped to shape her thinking. Chapters 2–3 contain discussions of critical topics such as the relationship between spirituality and religion, the question of life after death, the integration of science and spirituality, and the role of prayer. Chapters 4–9 offer methods of individual transformation. Various exercises are explained and discussed from Nightingale's perspective, and all are appropriate for both nurses and patients. Indeed, Nightingale wrote in *Notes on Nursing* (1860/1969), "The same laws of health or of nursing, for they are in reality the same, obtain among the well as among the sick" (p. 9). This text focuses on the nurse's perspective, however, for it is primarily our own experience that allows us to help others.

When writing about spirituality, word choices can be limiting. For example, following the custom of her era, Nightingale used the masculine pronoun to refer to God. She conceptualized God, however, as a *divine mind* or *universal spirit of right* that transcends all personal limitations, including gender. Also, terms used in this text such as "higher" and "deeper" are not meant to be taken literally but regarded as metaphors for a transcendent dimension of reality. As a three-dimensional cube includes and transcends a two-dimensional plane, the spiritual reality includes and transcends the three-dimensional realm of sensory reality. Nightingale's view, which is consistent with mystical writings of both Eastern and Western cultures, envisions the universal spirit of right as *both* the transcendent reality and the inner essence of every human being. Thus "developing" or "acquiring" spirituality actually mean allowing one's own true, or basic, nature to unfold.

The many short quotations from *Suggestions for Thought* in this text have been taken from the edited edition (Calabria & Macrae, 1994). In the original work, Nightingale was inconsistent in her use of capitalization, italics, and some other elements of punctuation.

All the passages in the edited edition were reproduced exactly as in the original, with all their inconsistencies.

I am most grateful for the guidance of Patricia L. Cleary, who served as editorial assistant. She contributed much to both the form and content of the manuscript. I am also very grateful to Ruth Chasek and the staff of Springer Publishing Company.

I would like to acknowledge the Theosophical Society in America, where I have studied comparative religion and philosophy, and the Division of Nursing at New York University, where I learned the principles of holistic nursing. These studies enabled me to appreciate Nightingale's spiritual views and their significance for the future of health care. I would also like to acknowledge Dora Kunz, who taught me, and many other nurses, how to enhance our spiritual awareness through meditation and the healing practice of therapeutic touch. Finally, I acknowledge the many nurses who are integrating Nightingale's ideas into their practice. It is for them, and for those who will do so in the future, that this book was written.

REFERENCES

Calabria, M., & Macrae, J. (Eds.). (1994). *Suggestions for thought by Florence Nightingale: Selections and commentaries.* Philadelphia: University of Pennsylvania Press. (Original work published 1860)

Cook, E. (1913). *The life of Florence Nightingale* (2 vols.). New York: Macmillan.

Nightingale, F. (1873a). A 'note' of interrogation. *Fraser's Magazine, 87,* 567–577.

Nightingale, F. (1873b). A sub-'note' of interrogation. *Fraser's Magazine,* 88, 25–36.

Nightingale, F. (1959). *Notes on nursing: What it is and what it is not.* New York: Dover Publications. (Original work published 1860)

I

Nightingale on Spirituality

1

Nightingale's Spiritual Vision

Florence Nightingale (1820–1910) was one of the best educated women of the 19th century. She was the younger of two daughters born to William Edward and Frances Smith Nightingale. Both parents came from wealthy British backgrounds. Her father was heir to an estate and her mother was the daughter of a philanthropic Member of Parliament. Frances (Fanny) Nightingale was a remarkably beautiful and generous woman whose major interest was high society. She possessed a touch of genius for organizing successful social functions. Florence inherited this organizational ability but, much to her mother's dismay, she used it to effect social reform rather than to gain social prestige.

William Edward Nightingale, a graduate of Cambridge University and a liberal-minded Unitarian, personally supervised the education of his daughters. He taught them philosophy, history, French, Italian, German, Latin and classical Greek. Florence was an eager student, but her sister Parthenope, who was of an artistic rather than intellectual bent, frequently rebelled. Pop, as she was called, "left her sister struggling with Greek verbs and joined her mother or escaped into the garden" (Woodham-Smith, 1950, p. 8).

By the time Florence was in her teens, she had mastered the elements of Greek and had translated portions of Plato's *Phaedo, Crito,* and *Apology* (Cook, 1913, p. 13). Plato's metaphysical philosophy greatly appealed to her and influenced her view of the world. Some of the main concepts in *Suggestions for Thought,* such as the material world being an imperfect expression of a higher, spiritual reality, can be traced back to Plato.

In Nightingale's later years, she helped her good friend Benjamin Jowett, Professor of Classics at Oxford University, revise his translations of Plato's dialogues. At his request, she annotated his summaries and introductions and offered numerous suggestions for revision. As the following passage from one of Jowett's letters indicates, he accepted Nightingale's help gratefully and also with a sense of humor:

> I cannot be too grateful to you for criticizing Plato . . . at the same time you are engaged in writing a pamphlet. I have adopted nearly all your hints as far as I have gone (however many hints I might give you, my belief is that you would never adopt any of them). (Quinn and Prest, 1987, p. 257)

Interestingly, Jowett's translations are still used in academic programs today, and thus students—many without realizing it—are being touched by Nightingale's mind.

Among William Nightingale's friends and acquaintances were scholars in the field of comparative religion, such as German orientalist Julius von Mohl and Prussian Egyptologist Baron Christian von Bunsen. Through her association with these individuals, Florence became exposed to the ideas that underlie different faiths such as Hinduism, Buddhism, Islam, and the religion of ancient Egypt. What impressed her were not the distinctions among faiths, but the similarities among their core teachings. While on a trip to Egypt and Greece in 1849, for example, she drew parallels between Pimander, a Hermetic text, and the Book of Genesis. "How like to one another are the highest beliefs in all spiritualized nations," she concluded (Calabria, 1997, p. 29).

THE INFLUENCE OF MEDIEVAL MYSTICS

There also were "curious analogies," Nightingale wrote to her friend Jowett, between the writings of Plato and those of the medieval Christian mystics (Cook, 1913, vol. 2, p. 232). All her life, Nightingale was drawn to the writings of the mystics—those individuals who have had direct experiences of the divine.

The term "mystic" is derived from the Latin *mysticus,* which means hidden. Through a change in consciousness, the mystic perceives reality from a higher or transcendent perspective that is hidden from ordinary sight. Cross-cultural studies of the mystical perspective reveal experiences of timelessness, of creative power, of profound love and compassion, of touching upon truth, and of union with God or a *transcendent reality* (Underhill, 1891/1974; Huxley, 1944; Cohen & Phipps, 1992).

In Nightingale's view, a mystical experience should not be considered an end in itself. It should serve as a source of wisdom, strength, and compassion so that we may better fulfill our purpose in the world (Dossey, 1999). Nightingale was a worker, and the active lives of the Western mystics appealed to her more than their more passive Eastern counterparts. In Underhill's (1891/1974) classic study of mysticism, we find that intense activity is one of the distinguishing characteristics of the Western mystical tradition. Underhill makes the critical point, however, that periods of solitude are necessary for active mystics as well as their reclusive counterparts. St. John of the Cross, St. Catherine of Sienna, St. Francis of Assisi, St. Teresa of Avila, and other active mystics have first retreated from the world to establish communion with the divine source"for in a quiet, undistracted state, the mind is better able to apprehend the underlying unity of life:

> It is true that in nearly every case such "great actives" have first left the world, as a necessary condition of establishing communion with that Absolute Life which reinforced their own; for a mind distracted by the many cannot apprehend the One. Hence something equivalent to the solitude of the wilderness is an essential part of mystical education. But, having established that communion, reordered their inner lives upon transcendent levels—being united with their Source not merely in temporary ecstasies, but in virtue of a permanent condition of the soul, they were impelled to abandon their solitude; and resumed, in some way, their contact with the world in order to become the medium whereby that Life flowed out to other men. To go up alone to the mountain and come back as an ambassador to the world, has ever been the method of humanity's best friends. This systole-and-diastole motion of retreat as the preliminary to a return remains the true ideal of Christian Mysticism in its highest development. (p. 173)

In Nightingale's later years she worked on a book of extracts from mystical writings which was to be titled *Notes from Devotional Authors of the Middle Ages, Collected, Chosen, and Freely Translated by Florence Nightingale*. Unfortunately, the book was never completed, but Sir Edward Cook (1913) was able to reconstruct the preface from her various notes and rough drafts. In the following passages she presents her view of mysticism and the spiritual life:

> For what is Mysticism? Is it not the attempt to draw near to God, not by rites or ceremonies, but by inward disposition? Is it not merely a hard word for "The Kingdom of Heaven is within"? Heaven is neither a place nor a time. There might be a Heaven not only *here* but *now*. . . . For all our actions, all our words, all our thoughts, the food upon which they are to live and have their being is to be the indwelling Presence of God, the union with God; that is, with the Spirit of Goodness and Wisdom.
>
> Where shall I find God? In myself. That is the true Mystical Doctrine. But then I myself must be in a state for Him to come and dwell in me. This is the whole aim of the Mystical Life; and all Mystical Rules in all times and countries have been laid down for putting the soul into such a state. (vol. 2, p. 233)

Interestingly, the main idea in the second paragraph above is echoed in these well known lines from Nightingale's *Notes on Nursing* (1860/1969): "Nature [i.e., the manifestation of God] alone cures . . . and what nursing has to do is to put the patient in the best condition for nature to act upon him" (p. 133).

Although Nightingale acknowledged the extraordinary individuals who are universally recognized as mystics, she did not feel they were specially gifted or chosen by God. In her view, every human being has the potential for mystical development. Indeed, the ultimate purpose of human life is to become one with the presence of God and to allow that presence to transform our thoughts and actions.

A NEW VISION FROM STATISTICS

William Nightingale was a member of the British Association for the Advancement of Science and often took his family to its meetings. Thus, from an early age, Florence was exposed to the latest developments in scientific thought. Having a natural predilection for collecting and analyzing data, she was deeply attracted to the developing field of statistical analysis. Cook (1913), her most authoritative biographer, called her a "passionate statistician." Her family said that she enjoyed reading statistical tables as most young women enjoy reading novels. As a young adult, Nightingale made such an extensive study of hospital and public health statistics that she became one of the leading experts in Europe.

While serving as Superintendent of Nurses during the Crimean War (1854–1856), Nightingale not only cared for the wounded, instituted sanitary reforms, and served as an auxiliary purveyor of hospital supplies, but also systematized the careless record-keeping practices of the military hospital. In a lengthy report entitled *Notes on Matters Affecting the Health, Efficiency and Hospital Administration of the British Army* (1858), she pioneered the graphical representation of statistics, illustrating with charts and diagrams how improved sanitation decreased the rate of mortality. This report served as the blueprint for extensive reforms introduced by the government after the war.

The study of statistics was, for Nightingale, not just an intellectual challenge and a means of effecting public health reform. It was also a sacred science. Unlike the scientific materialists of her day who held that scientific laws by themselves provided a complete understanding of the universe, Nightingale felt that an ordered universe was a reflection of a *higher intelligence*. As did Newton and Gallileo, she believed that the natural laws discovered by science are the *thoughts of God*. In *Suggestions for Thought* (1860/1994), she wrote that "if we could get rid of the word 'law,' we would, and substitute for it 'a thought of God.' For this is all that it means" (p. 39).

For Nightingale, the thoughts of God were revealed in the patterns of statistics. Thus the study of statistics may have been analogous to the mystical experience because it gave a higher perspective on reality, revealing hidden connections among apparently separate phenomena. Statistics revealed an interconnected and ordered universe—a reflection, she felt, of the *divine mind*.

In a universe organized by natural or scientific laws, nothing occurs in a vacuum. All events--physical, psychological, and spiritual—are either caused by, or correlated with, other events. Thus Nightingale thought that spiritual development could be approached scientifically, as a process regulated by law. In her view, "mystical rules in all times and countries" represent universal principles which, applied appropriately, can facilitate the indwelling of the divine life.

In *Suggestions for Thought* (1860/1994), Nightingale strongly took issue with those who felt that the spiritual dimension lay outside the realm of science. In the following passage, she poked fun at the imprecise nature of religious writings of her time:

> Scarcely a day passes but books, by the orthodox and the unortho-dox, by men and by women, are advertised, with titles as follows (I take these at random):—"Passing Thoughts on Religion," Musings on Manifestations of God to the Soul of Man." As for the "Impres-sions," the "Aspirations," their name is legion. Now, can we call this anything but *impertinence* to God? What should we say if we saw advertised, "Passing thoughts" on hydrostatics, "Musings" on clini-cal surgery, "Impressions" on life assurances? Everybody would laugh, and nobody would read the book. Is religion, confessedly the most important of all subjects, to be the only one on which anybody's *passing* thoughts are good enough? Is the nature of God the only science not worth study? I am not aware that any book called "*Fan-cies* on Religion" has yet appeared, but the title would be by no means a misnomer, for much that is written consists of nothing but fancies. (p. 7)

THE INFLUENCE OF ORGANIZED RELIGIONS

Unitarianism

Fanny Nightingale, like William Edward, came from a Unitarian background. Her father, William Smith, a prominent Unitarian member of Parliament, devoted himself to securing civil and legal rights for non-Anglican Protestants, Catholics, and Jews. He con-vinced Parliament in 1813 to pass the Unitarian Toleration Act, which made denying the divinity of Christ no longer a crime.

The Unitarians of the 19th century were characterized by their rejection of both the Trinity (Father, Son, and Holy Spirit) and the divinity of Christ. They also questioned such doctrines as original sin, the atonement, the last judgment, and eternal damnation. Although many based their beliefs on scripture, others looked to human reason and conscience rather than to scripture or church authority. Social causes such as prison reform, education, temperance, and women's rights were central to the work of the Unitarian community (Edwards, 1984).

Because social prestige rather than reform was a top priority for Fanny, she abandoned the Unitarian Church and raised her two daughters in the Church of England. Despite Florence's Anglican upbringing, however, she held many beliefs in common with the Unitarians and, like them, she felt that one's actions were the ultimate test of one's spiritual development (Widerquist, 1992). In *Suggestions for Thought* (1860/1994) she wrote that "unless you make a life which shall be the manifestation of your religion, it does not much signify what you believe" (p. 116).

The Broad Church

Ideas consistent with Unitarianism entered the mid-19th century Anglican Church through the *Broad Church* movement (Wigmore-Beddes, 1971). The Broad Church was composed of a group of liberal Anglicans who, although differing on specific theological issues, were united by their critical approach to both doctrine and scripture and by their belief in freedom of inquiry. Like Unitarians, the individuals comprising the Broad Church sought to emphasize the ethical dimension of Christianity. They challenged some church doctrines, such as original sin, eternal damnation, and Christ's atonement for humanity's sins, and also questioned whether the Bible was divinely inspired. Broad Churchmen generally held that great spiritual truths had been imparted to humanity throughout the course of history, and thus were not exclusive to Christianity.

Nightingale's friend, Benjamin Jowett, a prominent member of the Broad Church, expressed the need for critical evaluation of scripture in *Essays and Reviews* (1860), a collection of writings by Broad Churchmen:

Any true doctrine of inspiration must conform to all well-ascertained facts of history or of science. The same fact cannot be true in religion when seen by the light of faith, and untrue in science when looked at through the medium of evidence or experiment. (p. 348)

Nightingale's thinking had much in common with that of the Broad Church (Calabria & Macrae, 1994). Like the Broad Church-men, Nightingale believed in freedom of inquiry in all religious matters. She, too, wanted religion held to the same critical standard as science, philosophy, and history. Her study of statistics revealed a universe regulated by divine or natural law, and thus she questioned religious beliefs that appeared to her to be contradictory to scientific law.

Roman Catholicism

Despite the fact that Nightingale remained a lifelong member of the Church of England, she was drawn, in her early adulthood, to the Roman Catholic orders, especially those devoted to serving the sick and the poor. She felt that the training they offered women was far superior to that of the Church of England:

For what training is there [in the Church of England] compared to that of the Catholic nun? . . . there is nothing like the training (in these days) which the Sacred Heart or the Order of St. Vincent gives to women. (Vicinus & Nergaard, 1989, p. 59)

During a 6-month visit to Rome when she was 27 years old, Nightingale went on a 10-day retreat at the convent of the Trinita de Monte. There she met the Madre Santa Columba, whose influence affected her for years thereafter. Tempted to convert to Catholicism, Nightingale discussed her situation with her friend, Rev. Henry Manning, who had recently converted from the Anglican to the Catholic Church. Manning was at first sympathetic, but after reading a 29-page proof of *Suggestions for Thought,* he advised her not to convert because her views were far too radical. In the following passage from a letter to Manning, Nightingale revealed that her deeply held spiritual views, which were not consistent with the orthodox teachings of the Catholic Church, prevented her from converting and joining a religious order:

I belong as little to the Ch. of England as to that of Rome—or rather my heart belongs as much to the Catholic Ch. as to that of England—oh, how much more. The only difference is that the former insists peremptorily upon my believing what I cannot believe, while the latter is too careless and indifferent to know whether I believe it or not. She proclaims out of the Prayer book what we are to believe, but she does not care whether we do (and we don't) while the Catholic Church examines into the fact. If it were not for that, I might have a home where now I have none. (Vicinus & Nergaard, pp. 59–60)

FAMILY AND SOCIAL CONSTRAINTS

Nightingale probably felt that she had no true home because she was so unhappy in her immediate family circle. She was bored and frustrated with her family's luxurious lifestyle, traveling between two country estates and entertaining lavishly. Fanny, a superb hostess, was determined that her two daughters would shine in society and marry well. But her mother's efforts meant little to Florence, who wrote that she "craved for some regular occupation, for something worth doing, instead of frittering time away on useless trifles" (Woodham-Smith, 1951, p. 9).

A regular occupation, however, was difficult to obtain for an upper-class English woman of the 19th century. Women were barred from enrolling in a university or entering any of the learned professions. Nursing was not considered a profession at that time. Training in the care of the ill was provided to members of some religious orders. Secular nursing, such as that offered in city hospitals, was considered menial work that required almost no training at all. Caregivers were frequently recruited from the ranks of street women, among whom alcoholism and promiscuity were common.

Florence's impassioned request to apprentice at the Salisbury Infirmary, a well-known hospital where Dr. Fowler, a family friend, was the head physician, was adamantly refused (Woodham-Smith, 1951). Fanny, angry and terrified that her daughter would have an affair with a "low, vulgar surgeon," wept that Florence was trying to "disgrace herself." Parthenope responded to the notion of Florence working in a hospital by becoming hysterical. William Edward, disgusted and upset at all the commotion, retreated to his London club. Woodam-Smith wrote that he made no attempt to conceal his disappointment: "Was it for this he had educated a charming daughter? Was this to be the end of the Latin and the Greek, the poetry and the philosophy, the Italian tour and the Paris frocks" (Woodham-Smith, 1951, p. 38)?

Unfortunately for Florence, there were only two proper choices for a young woman in her class of society: to stay at home and be subject to the will of her parents until they died, or to marry and have her inheritance pass on to her husband. Neither was satisfactory for Florence. She found little fulfillment at home and spent as much time away as possible. To her mother's bitter disappointment, she refused an offer of marriage from Richard Moncton Milnes (Lord Houghton). Although she loved him, she indicated in a private note that his lifestyle would not satisfy her need to find her own path:

> I have an intellectual nature which requires satisfaction and that would find it in him. I have a passionate nature which requires satisfaction and that at would find it in him. I have a moral, an active, nature which requires satisfaction and that would not find it in his life. . . .
>
> I know I could not bear his life, that to be nailed to a continuation, an exaggeration of my present life without hope of another would be intolerable to me—that voluntarily to put it out of my power ever to be able to seize the chance of forming for myself a true and rich life would seem to me like suicide. (Woodham-Smith, 1951, pp. 51–52)

Nightingale finally gained her freedom in 1853 when she was 33 years old. She accepted, without parental permission, an unpaid position as Superintendent of the Institution for the Care of Sick Gentlewomen in Distressed Circumstances. She thought this facility might be acceptable to the family because it was owned and operated by the Anglican Church. Although her mother and sister exploded in anger, her father relented and provided her with an independent income. Her position was thus secured, and she was able to take up residence at the Institution. One year later, when the Crimean War broke out, she was asked by the British Secretary at War to serve as Superintendent of Nurses in the military hospitals.

Interestingly, Nightingale's spiritual views became apparent soon after she assumed her post at the Institution for the Care of Sick Gentlewomen. Until her appointment, only members of the Church of England could be admitted to the facility. Against great odds she persuaded the administrative committee to change this policy so that women of all faiths could be admitted and their clergy could be free to attend them. In a letter to a friend, Nightingale expressed frustration with the way she was expected to administer this policy when non-Anglican clergy visited:

> So now it is settled, and *in print* that we are to take in all denominations whatever, and allow them to be visited by their respective priests and Muftis, provided that *I* will receive (in any case *whatsoever* that is *not* of the Church of England) the obnoxious animal at the door, take him upstairs myself, remain while he is conferring with his patient, make myself *responsible* that he does not speak to, or look at, *anyone else,* and bring him downstairs again in a noose, and out into the street. And to this I have agreed! And this is in print! Amen! (quoted in Woodham-Smith, 1951, p. 75)

Unfortunately, Nightingale never completely resolved her family difficulties, and they took a toll on her health for the greater part of her life. Sir George Pickering (1974) theorizes that the conflict between fulfilling her mission in life and fulfilling her family's expectations was the cause of the chronic illness that plagued Nightingale after her return from the Crimean War. In his study of creative individuals who suffered from ill health, Pickering describes Nightingale's condition as a "psychoneurosis":

> It would be hard to find a more classical case. Attacks of breathlessness, palpitations, giddiness, induced by unwanted events or events that cause apprehension, are typical and this is what Miss Nightingale displayed. Her illness prevented her from seeing unwanted visitors, and her mother and sister in particular, who would have wasted so much of her time. . . .

. . . Moreover, because it was now apparent that an unwelcome visitor would bring on an attack, all visits had to be by appointment and such was her delicate health that some could not be arranged at all. This enabled her to plan her time so that she could use it in the way she desired and in that way only. . . .

. . . She worked with great concentration and efficiency for some sixteen hours a day. She expected her colleagues and helpers to do likewise. And such was the magic of her legend and the power of her personality that they did. (pp. 171–172)

An examination of the broader clinical picture, however, suggests that the family conflict may have aggravated rather than caused Nightingale's illness. Young (1995) and Dossey (1998, 1999) provide persuasive evidence that Nightingale's reported symptoms are compatible with Mediterranean fever, caused by the bacterium Brucella. It was one of several fevers commonly identified by British army doctors during the Crimean War, and a disease that is still endemic today in many parts of underdeveloped countries. Relapses are common, and the term "chronic brucellosis" is used when the disease lasts longer than a year.

Nightingale had a severe attack of fever during her stay in the Crimea, and for the next 30 years suffered bouts of symptoms that were characteristic of brucellosis. Besides the dyspnea, tachycardia, and palpitations mentioned by Pickering, Nightingale also suffered from fever, generalized weakness, laryngitis, anorexia, insomnia, severe sciatic pain, joint pain, paralysis of the lower extremities, irritability, and depression. The fact that she continued to lead a life of great public service despite these debilitating symptoms makes her one of the most remarkable women in history.

A DIVINE CALLING

Nightingale's family difficulties were intensified by the fact that, when she was 16 years old, she experienced the first of several "inner awakenings." She did not describe the experience in great detail; she simply noted that on February 7, 1837, God spoke to her and called her to his service. The divine voice did not give her specific instructions, only a powerful "inner certainty" that her life was to be devoted to God's service.

The years following Nightingale's initial call were difficult. As we discussed previously, her mother and sister continually thwarted her attempts to engage in hospital work, to which she was particularly drawn. She painfully realized that the lifestyle of the man she loved was not compatible with her inner calling. Joining a religious order dedicated to service would have provided Nightingale with an outlet for her creative energy. However, many of the beliefs held by these orders were not compatible with her personal views, which were extremely radical for her time.

Nightingale also had to confront her "demons," that is, those personal characteristics she felt would not be consistent with a spiritually oriented life, such as her excessive daydreaming and her desire for power and recognition. Nightingale's internal struggles are poignantly recorded in personal notes and also in a diary she kept during a trip to Egypt in 1849 (Calabria, 1997). In the diary she expressed her profound feelings of guilt for creating disharmony in her family, that is, for not being contented with a life of wealth and privilege. She wrestled with a tendency for what she called "dreaming," or leaving the immediacy of the moment in trance-like fantasies. Her habit of "dreaming" was most probably a reaction to her family's social routine, from which she longed to escape. Acknowledging her desire for personal power and recognition, Nightingale remembered the words of the Madre Santa Columba, whom she met at the Trinita in Rome: "My Madre said to me Can you hesitate between the God of the whole earth and your little reputation" (Calabria, 1997, p. 46)?

Despite her internal struggles and the lack of support from her family, Nightingale exhibited extraordinary courage and determination in her attempt to honor her spiritual calling. As Superintendent of Nurses during the Crimean War, for example, her single-minded devotion and energy were prodigious. She took care of the most serious cases herself and appeared to follow intuitive guidance in locating them. A physician who observed her at work reported:

> I believe that there was never a severe case of any kind that escaped her notice, and sometimes it was wonderful to see her at the bedside

of a patient who had been admitted perhaps but an hour before, and of whose arrival one would hardly have supposed it possible she could be already cognizant. (quoted in Cook, 1913, vol. 1, p. 236)

Cook (1913) quotes General Bentinck, who said that Nightingale had been known to pass eight hours on her knees dressing wounds and administering comfort:

There were times when she stood for twenty hours at a stretch, apportioning quarters, distributing stores, directing the labours of her staff, or assisting at the painful operations where her presence might sooth or support. (vol. 1, p. 235)

In the Crimea, Nightingale demonstrated not only administrative genius and clinical expertise, but also a therapeutic presence. A contemporary writer described the influence of her presence on the soldiers:

The magic of her power over men was felt in the room—the dreaded, the blood-stained room—where operations took place. There perhaps the maimed soldier, if not yet resigned to his fate, might at first be craving death rather than meet with the knife of the surgeon; but, when such a one looked and saw that the honored Lady-in-Chief was patiently standing beside him, and—with lips closely set and hands folded—decreeing herself to go through the pain of witnessing pain, he used to fall into the mood for obeying her silent command, and—finding strange support in her presence—bring himself to submit and endure. (quoted in Cook, 1913, vol. 1, p. 238)

A SPIRITUAL FOUNDATION FOR NURSING

Nightingale believed that the physical body is not the essence or eternal dimension of human nature, and yet she spent her life trying to improve environmental conditions and physical health. From her point of view, the purpose of human existence is to create "heaven upon the earth," that is, to consciously bring the material world into complete harmony with the divine. "The 'Kingdom of Heaven is within,' " she wrote, "but we must also make it without" (Nightingale, 1873). For her, the physical body is the vehicle of the spirit, the means by which the eternal spirit performs its work in the world.

Nursing and Natural Law

Because Nightingale believed that the universe is regulated by natural laws, or *thoughts of God,* she felt that health promotion must occur through the discovery and proper application of universal principles. She wrote emphatically against the concept, prevalent in her time, that illness arises as an arbitrary punishment for sinful behavior. Illness, from her perspective, implies an ignorance of natural law. For example, if the laws of sanitation are not observed, she wrote, cholera will exist among both saints and sinners alike. In the passage below from *Suggestions for Thought* (1860/1994), she comments on the story of the blind man in the New Testament:

> "Did this man sin or his parents?"
> That question implied a false idea. Sin regards those laws which concern our spiritual and moral being, that is, our feelings and wills towards God and our fellow creatures. That a man is born blind implies some ignorance of physical law, either on his own part or on that of those who preceded him.
> Those physical laws may have been disregarded in consequence of something wrong in the spiritual life. Disease in the spiritual being will often lead to indulgence in malpractices in the physical. But the immediate cause of blindness is a physical law. And it is untrue to regard physical evil as a punishment, that is, an arbitrary infliction for some spiritual evil. (p. 82)

Many of Nightingale's recommendations for the care of the body are contained in her classic text, *Notes on Nursing* (1860/1969). Although her text is focused on the care of patients, Nightingale makes the important statement that the basic principles of health are universal laws and thus apply to the well and the sick:

> The same laws of health or of nursing, for they are in reality the same, obtain among the well as among the sick. The breaking of them produces only a less violent consequence among the former than among the latter,—and this sometimes, not always. (pp. 9–10)

The central theme of *Notes on Nursing (1860/1969)*, which Nightingale emphasized in capital letters, is that the nurse must keep the air in the patient's room as pure as the outside air, without chilling him (p. 12). From her perspective, disease is a reparative process that involves an elimination of toxins from the body. Ventilation is essential because a free flow of air prevents a buildup of toxins in the patient's immediate environment. Sanitation is equally important: the patient should be bathed frequently, as toxins are released through the skin as well as through the lungs, and all soiled material should be taken immediately out of the sickroom.

As the body requires "vital power" to perform the work of healing, conserving and enhancing energy is a central part of Nightingale's approach to nursing. She emphasized that the patient must be kept warm, have access to sunlight, be given proper nourishment at the time he or she can best tolerate it, and be protected from external disturbances such as unnecessary noise.

For Nightingale, the promotion of psychological health, as well as physical health, is a lawful process. "To think we can be good under any circumstances is like thinking that we may be healthy when we are living over a sewer" (*Suggestions for Thought*, 1860/ 1994, p. 123). Nightingale's views on psychological and social behavior were deeply influenced by the work of Adolph Quetelet (1796– 1874), the Belgian natural scientist who is regarded as the founder of modern social statistics (Cook, 1913). Applying statistical methods, Quetelet demonstrated yearly regularities in the age-specific crime rates for both men and women in various countries and in different social groups. He felt, as did Nightingale, that these regularities were caused by the social conditions of these groups. Thus legislation which improved social conditions would also improve human behavior, and the probability of crime would be lowered.

Nightingale applied this theory in her attempt to control the widespread abuse of alcohol among the convalescent soldiers in the Crimean hospital. She observed that the soldiers were bored and spent money on drink because they mistrusted the official means of sending their paychecks home. In response to this situation, Nightingale instituted and personally supervised an alternative means whereby the soldiers could send money home to their families and also supervised the establishment of a library, a school, and a recreational program. The positive response to Nightingale's efforts shocked not only the military establishment, but also the nation. Woodham-Smith (1957) wrote:

> It was an astonishing achievement, and during the winter of 1855–56 the picture of the British soldier as a drunken intractable brute faded away never to return. "She taught," said an eye-witness, "officers and officials to treat the soldiers as Christian men." (p. 168)

God's Presence in the World

Nightingale had a profound sense of God's immanence, or presence, within the world. For her, the ordered beauty of nature is "the continuous manifestation of God's presence" (*Suggestion for Thought*, 1860/1994, p. 41). She also felt that God was present within humanity. Great scientific discoveries, acts of compassion and courage, the highest forms of artistic expression were, to her, the divine spirit manifesting on earth.

Nightingale was not a pantheist (that is, someone who *equates* nature with God), for she believed that the divine spirit not only permeates, but also transcends the created world. Indeed, in her view the whole of nature—at any moment in time—is only a *partial* manifestation of the boundless creativity of the mind of God.

It was Nightingale's sense of divinity *within* the world, however, that gave her work in nursing a profound sense of meaning. If nature is the manifestation of God, then cooperating with nature, by facilitating the healing process, is also cooperating with God. She wrote in *Notes on Nursing* that "God lays down certain physical laws. Upon his carrying out such laws depends our responsibility" (p. 25). For Nightingale, nursing was a means of harmonizing oneself with the divine source of all existence and, thus, it was a sacred process.

REFERENCES

Calabria, M. (1997). *Florence Nightingale in Egypt and Greece*. Albany, NY: State University of New York Press.

Calabria, M., & Macrae, J. (Eds.) (1994). *Suggestions for thought by Florence Nightingale: Selections and commentaries.* Philadelphia: University of Pennsylvania Press.

Cook, E. (1913). *The life of Florence Nightingale* (2 vols.). London: Macmillan.

Dossey, B. (1998). Florence Nightingale: Her Crimean fever and chronic illness. *Journal of Holistic Nursing, 16,* 168–196.

Dossey, B. (1998). Florence Nightingale: A 19th century mystic. *Journal of Holistic Nursing, 16,* 111–163.

Dossey, B. (1999). *Florence Nightingale: Mystic, visionary, and healer.* Springhouse, PA: Springhouse.

Edwards, D. L. (1983). *Christian England: From the eighteenth century to the First World War (vol. 3).* Grand Rapids, MI: William B. Eerdmans.

Huxley, A. (1945). *The perennial philosophy.* New York: Harper and Row.

Jowett, B. (1860). On the interpretation of scripture. In *Essays and reviews.* London: John W. Parker and Son.

Nightingale, F. (1860/1969). *Notes on nursing: What it is, and what it is not.* New York: Dover Publications.

Nightingale, F. (1873). A sub-'note' of interrogation. *Fraser's Magazine, 88,* 25–36.

Pickering, G. (1974). *Creative malady.* New York: Oxford University Press.

Quinn, E. V., & Prest, J. M. (1987). *Dear Miss Nightingale: A selection of Benjamin Jowett's letters: 1860–1893.* Oxford: Clarendon Press.

Underhill, E. (1891/1974). *Mysticism: A study in the development of man's spiritual consciousness.* New York: Penguin.

Vicinis, M., & Nergaard, B. (Eds.). (1990). *Ever yours, Florence Nightingale: Selected letters.* Cambridge: Harvard University Press.

Widerquist, J. (1992). The spirituality of Florence Nightingale. *Nursing Research, 41,* 49–55.

Woodham-Smith, C. (1951). *Florence Nightingale: 1820–1910.* New York: McGraw-Hill.

Wigmore-Beddes, D. (1971). *Yesterday's radicals: A study of the affinity between Unitarianism and Broad Church Anglicanism in the nineteenth century.* Cambridge: James and Clarke.

Young, D. A. B. (1995). Florence Nightingale's fever. *British Medical Journal, 311,* 1697–1700.

2

Spirituality, Religion, and Health Care

From Nightingale's perspective, spirituality is an experiential phenomenon; it is the consciousness of a divine presence. In the following passage from *Suggestions for Thought* (1860/ 1994), she made distinctions among the spiritual, the intellectual, and the humanistic:

What do we mean by spirituality?

Is it not feeling, as distinct from both intellect and from the affection of one human being to another? We do not call love, admiration, reverence, for a human being, spirituality, nor the trust which one human being has in another. These we call humanizing influences; but feelings called forth by the consciousness of a presence of higher nature than human, unconnected with the material, these we call spiritual influences; and this we are conscious is the highest capability of our nature. Whenever we love, admire, reverence, trust this higher presence—whenever we sympathize with, partake in the purpose, thought, feeling, of this highest presence—these are our best moments.

Sympathy with man, interest in any right or innocent object, is not excluded by this higher state, is never indeed perfectly right and healthy, except in connexion with it. (p. 120)

For Nightingale, spirituality is not an intellectual belief, but an actual experience. Saying "I believe in God" is different from saying "I feel the divine presence in my life." She felt that experience, rather than belief by itself, is the transformative element. Ideally, belief should facilitate the development of spiritual experience but, as we shall discuss subsequently, such is not always the case.

DISTINGUISHING SPIRITUALITY FROM RELIGION

Spirituality, in Nightingale's view, is the experience of our unity with the divine power and consciousness that underlies the created world. Religion, a system of beliefs and practices, ideally should serve to enhance and express the experience of spirituality. Religion is a means, and spirituality is the end. The essence of religion, Nightingale wrote in *Suggestions for Thought* (1860/1994), is "the tie, the *binding,* or connexion between the Perfect and the imperfect, the eternal and the temporal, the infinite and the finite, the universal and the individual" (p. 23).

Miller (1997), in his article on the spiritual aspects of addiction treatment, articulates in modern terminology a view of the relationship between spirituality and religion that is consistent with Nightingale's:

Although one can talk about spirituality in a way that refers only to personal characteristics such as values and morals, for the author, the term has no meaning unless it refers to a transcendent dimension outside of material existence, one that can definitely be experienced, but never bounded, controlled, or possessed. To speak of the spiritual is to speak of one's relationship to that which is outside oneself, beyond material existence; what is referred to generically in AA as a Higher Power. Religion, on the other hand, is defined by its boundaries, by beliefs, practices, and structures. It is an organized search for the spiritual. Looked at in this way, spirituality cannot, by definition, be subsumed or bounded within religion. Rather, religion is one means toward spirituality. As it is popular to say these days, one can be spiritual without being religious. The great spiritual teachers also warn us that it is quite possible to be so religious or pious as to miss the spiritual altogether. (p. 39)

Although Nightingale accepted all the traditional means of developing spirituality, such as the observation of the Sabbath, participation in rituals and services, the study of the Bible and other sacred texts, receiving the sacraments, etc., she was deeply aware that organized religion was not the only means of developing spiritual awareness. Indeed, she felt that the study of nature's laws through statistical analysis was religious because it helped to align her mind with the universal mind of God. Compassionate service was also religious, because it deepened her experience of the unity of all life.

A famous example of non-traditional spirituality can be found in the life and writings of Henry Thoreau, the American naturalist and philosopher. Although he did not attend church regularly, he studied the great scriptures of both Eastern and Western traditions. He felt, very profoundly, that the divine was manifest in nature, and that by living in harmony with nature one could participate in the divine life. On Thoreau's deathbed, his Aunt Louisa asked him if he had made his peace with God. "I did not know we had ever quarreled, Aunt," he replied (Richardson, 1986, p. 389).

RELIGIOUS BELIEF AND EXPERIENCE

Believing Is Seeing

Although we can make an intellectual distinction between spirituality as the goal and religion as a means, the boundaries between spirituality and religion become much less distinct in our actual experience. The reason for this lack of clear distinction is that the experience of that which can be "never bounded, controlled or possessed" is interpreted and shaped, to a greater or lesser degree, by religious beliefs and practices based upon these beliefs. "Wherever miracles have been believed," Nightingale wrote in *Suggestions for Thought* (1860/1994), "they have been seen" (p. 51). This is a critical point that Nightingale raised, but did not elaborate upon, in her spiritual writings.

An interesting example of the way spiritual experiences are interpreted by existing beliefs can be found in the literature on near-death experiences. Individuals who have clinically died and subsequently regained physical consciousness sometimes report having encountered a spiritual *being of light*. Raymond Moody (1975), who pioneered the research in this area, wrote that the identification of this being tends to be a function of the individual's religious perspective:

> What is perhaps the most incredible common element in the accounts I have studied, and is certainly the element which has the

most profound effect upon the individual, is the encounter with a very bright light. Typically, at its first appearance, this light is dim, but it rapidly gets brighter until it reaches an unearthly brilliance. Yet . . . many make the specific point that it does not in any way hurt their eyes, or dazzle them, or keep them from seeing other things around them.

Despite the light's unusual manifestation, however, not one person has expressed any doubt whatsoever that it was a being, a being of light. Not only that, it is a personal being. It has a very definite personality. The love and the warmth which emanate from this being to the dying person are utterly beyond words, and he feels completely surrounded by it and taken up in it. . . .

Interestingly, while the above description of the being of light is utterly invariable, the identification of the being varies from individual to individual and seems to be largely a function of the religious background, training, or beliefs of the person involved. Thus, most of those who are Christian in training or belief identify the light as Christ and sometimes draw Biblical parallels in support of their interpretation. A Jewish man and woman identified the light as an "angel. . .". A man who had had no religious beliefs or training at all prior to his experience simply identified what he saw as "a being of light." (pp. 58–59)

We not only interpret our experiences by our beliefs, our beliefs can actually shape our experiences. In clinical practice the *self-fulfilling prophesy* illustrates the fact that beliefs influence life experience. For example, if a patient believes that an event will turn out bad, there is, unfortunately, a high probability that it will. If beliefs influence our experience at the sensory level, how much more so must they influence our experience of the nontangible, mysterious domain of the spirit?

We might ask if it is possible to suspend all religious beliefs and directly experience the divine reality. This is a difficult issue because, throughout human history, access to the spiritual realms has been gained primarily through religious rituals and through the practice of various disciplines such as yoga, zazen, and contemplative prayer. These disciplines, based on cultural and religious beliefs, give structure to our experience of that which can be "never bounded, controlled, or possessed." Goleman (1977) in his comparative analysis of meditation methods, writes that the "method is the seed of the goal: the contours of the state the meditator reaches depends on how he arrived" (p. 114).

Religious Belief and Physical Health

Beliefs not only shape our experience of the external world, they also affect our experience of the internal world, that is, our emotions and physical processes. In health care, the effect of belief on the physical body is universally recognized in the placebo effect, which is elicited by belief and expectation on the part of the patient and/or on the part of the provider. Because belief influences treatment outcomes, clinical research, to be considered valid, must control for the placebo effect.

Psychiatrist Viktor Frankl, incarcerated in a Nazi concentration camp during World War II, observed that a prisoner's belief in the future and sense of purpose in life were major factors in determining his or her survival. In his well-known book *Man's Search for Meaning* (1959) he told of a friend who dreamed of being released on March 30th. The promised date arrived and the camp was not liberated. The friend suddenly took ill on March 29th, ran a high fever and died on March 31st. "To all outward appearances," Frankl wrote, "he had died of typhus" (p. 96).

> The prisoner who had lost faith in the future—his future—was doomed. With his loss of belief in the future, he also lost his spiritual hold; he let himself decline and became subject to mental and physical decay. . . .
> Those who know how close the connection is between the state of mind of a man—his courage and hope, or lack of them—and the state of immunity of his body, will understand that the sudden loss of hope and courage can have a deadly effect. The ultimate cause of my friend's death was that the expected liberation did not come and he was severely disappointed. This suddenly lowered his body's resistance against the latent typhus infection. His faith in the future and will to live had become paralyzed and his body fell victim to illness— and thus the voice of his dream was right after all. (pp. 95, 96–97)

Religious beliefs are particularly powerful because they can provide a sense of meaning and purpose to human existence. Human beings are the only animals on earth with a high degree of self-awareness and the ability to reflect on their own mortality. The belief that life has no absolute meaning—that we live, love, suffer and triumph over obstacles, only to become extinct at death—can be so stressful and health-impairing that Herbert Benson (1996), one of the leading researchers in mind/body medicine, writes that human beings are genetically "wired for God" to enhance their well-being and survival:

> Cicero is reported to have said, "All philosophy only talks about one thing—death." I have come to believe that in order to counter this fundamental angst, humans are also wired for God. Whether or not God exists, our genes guarantee that we will bear faith and that our bodies will be soothed by believing in some antithesis to mortality and human frailty. So that we will not be incapacitated by the acknowledgement and dread of death, our brains harbor beliefs in a better, nobler meaning to life. (p. 198)

Whether or not belief in God is genetically based, scientific research supports the thesis that religious beliefs can have a positive effect on health. In a comprehensive review of studies on the medical effects of religious beliefs and practices, Matthews et al. (1993) found that religious factors were associated with reduced alcohol, cigarette, and drug use; reduced anxiety, depression, and hostility; reduced blood pressure; improved quality of life in patients with heart disease; and improved general health.

A RESPECT FOR ALL FAITHS

Because religious beliefs (and practices based upon them) shape, to a greater or lesser degree, our experience of spirituality, we may never be able to separate *completely* the concepts of spirituality and religion. However, we can become aware of the basic distinction—spirituality being the goal and religion being a means—and refrain from equating these two concepts.

From Nightingale's perspective, it is of the utmost importance that we refrain from equating spirituality with one particular religion. Viewing God *solely* from one religious perspective can hinder spiritual growth in two ways: (a) by limiting our understanding of spirituality and (b) by creating divisiveness among religious groups, which is the antithesis of the unitive spiritual reality.

Nightingale's study of comparative religion, particularly the mystical element, led her to conclude that spirituality is not the property of any one religious tradition; it is part of human nature, the highest level of human consciousness. She felt that every religious tradition offers unique insights. For example, although she planned to include only Christian writings in her book on mysticism, she wrote in a letter that the topic cannot be fully understood without a comprehensive study: "You must go to Mahometanism, to Buddhism, to the East, to the Sufis & Fakirs, to Pantheism, for the right growth of mysticism" (*Calendar of Letters*, 3, C14,659).

Nightingale read all the literature on comparative religion that was available in England, and also gathered information on her trips abroad. Calabria (1990) wrote that Nightingale, on her voyage to Egypt, understood and appreciated the ancient view of good and evil as complementary processes in a dynamic universe. In one of her letters from Egypt, Nightingale commented on a depiction in a temple:

> It was the Great Ramses crowned by the good and evil principle on either side. What a deep philosophy!—what theory of the world has ever gone farther than this? The evil is not the opposer of the good, but its *collaborateur*—the left hand of God as good is his right. . . . The king at his entrance to life is initiated into the belief that what we call the evil was the giver of life and power as well as the good. . . .
> The old Egyptians believed that out of good came forth evil, and out of evil came forth good; or as I should translate it, out of the well ordered comes forth the inharmonious, the passionate; and out of disorder again order; and both are a benefit. (Sattin, 1987, p. 96)

Ideally, an appreciation for the insights and practices of other faiths would help to create harmony among religious groups and also bring us closer to the spiritual reality that transcends all perspectives. Circumstances, however, are not always ideal. Nightingale's experience in the Crimea illustrates the degree to which religious divisiveness can impede a spiritual cause. Cook (1913) wrote at length about her "religious difficulties":

> It was not enough that such a mission as hers was conceived in the very spirit of the Founder of Christianity: "I was sick and ye visited me." The question was eagerly and angrily canvassed under which of the rival Christian banners the visitation of the sick soldiers should be, and was being carried on. . . . I am not sure that of all her difficulties the religious one was not the most wearing and worrying, as it was also assuredly the most unnecessary and the least excusable. It engulfed a noble undertaking in a fog of envy, strife, and futile railing. (vol. 1, p. 244)

As we discussed in chapter 1, Nightingale's mission to the Crimea was sponsored by the British government. The plan, developed by the Secretary at War and approved by Nightingale, was for the party of nurses to represent all the leading religious sects. For effective nursing administration during a time of war, Nightingale was to be given central authority over all nurses in the party. However, the authorities at Devonshire Square, one of the foremost Protestant institutions, refused to accept Nightingale's central control. Because of this decision, the Devonshire Square nurses could not be accepted. The party thus had a preponderance of Roman Catholics and High Church Anglicans, a situation which evoked a loud public outcry.

Referring to the commotion caused by the religious issue, Parthenope Nightingale wrote:

> We are only vexed because Flo so earnestly desired to include all shades of opinion, to prove that all, however they differed, might work together in a common brotherhood of love to God and man. (quoted in Cook, 1913, vol. 1, p. 159)

Nightingale was continually pressured to balance the numbers by accepting women based on religious denomination rather than experience and expertise in nursing. In a note on some of her staff (quoted in Cook, 1913) Nightingale wrote:

> Excellent, gentle, self-devoted women fit more for heaven than for a Hospital, they flit about like angels without hands among the patients,

and soothe their souls, while they leave their bodies dirty and neglected. They never complain, they are eager for self-mortification. But I came not to mortify the nurses, but to nurse the wounded. (vol. 1, p. 246)

In many instances, soothing the souls of the wounded soldiers took the form of proselytism. Numerous charges and countercharges of proselytism were referred by the chaplains to the Secretary of State, who replied that he deeply lamented the fact that religious differences had arisen to such an extent "as to mar the united energies and labours" of those who dedicated themselves to the care of the wounded.

In the latter part of the twentieth century we have not seen widespread proselytizing in the hospitals. On the contrary, we have seen a reluctance on the part of caregivers to deal with religious matters. A nurse might say: "Religion is a personal concern. I have strong religious beliefs, but I have no right to impose these on the patients. In my work I must respect their integrity." Another might give a different reason: "I have no strong religious beliefs. I feel that the goodness of life is mixed with so much suffering that I doubt much of what I was taught as a child. I'm not comfortable with religious issues and I'd like to keep them out of patient care."

Because patients are sensitive to their caregivers' attitudes, they also tend to keep silent. And this silence is unhealthy because it impedes the expansion of nursing knowledge. It is only very recently, for example, that near-death experiences have been openly discussed, documented, and evaluated for their therapeutic value (Moody, 1975; Ring, 1982).

If spirituality could be viewed as a dimension of human consciousness that transcends the confines of separate religious traditions, we, as nurses, might feel less inhibited in this area. We might encourage our patients to share their inner spiritual experiences and then a wealth of valuable material could emerge from the silence.

FREEDOM OF BELIEF

In a previous section we discussed the idea that religious beliefs provide a sense of meaning and purpose in life which, through the mind/body connection, enhances physical health and well-being. From Nightingale's perspective, however, the purpose of religious belief is to facilitate spiritual development. Our beliefs should not only comfort us, they should help bring us closer to truth. Because of her scientific approach to spirituality, Nightingale did not feel that any one religious text or set of beliefs represented ultimate truth. She considered religious beliefs as working hypotheses which require rigorous testing. In *Suggestions for Thought* (1860/1994) she wrote:

> Much is to be learnt from the Bible, and probably from all books which have been accepted by large portions of mankind as inspired; but man's capabilities of observation, thought, and feeling exercised on the universe, past, present, and to come, are the source of religious knowledge. (p. 126)

When a belief helps its followers develop spirituality it should be retained. When it does not, it should be re-evaluated or discarded. For example, Nightingale challenged the Biblical idea that poverty brings us closer to God. She saw in her statistical tables that, for the general population, poverty correlated with crime, disease, and high mortality rates.

The objection can be raised that monastic communities, whose ultimate goal is spiritual development, frequently require a vow of poverty. In these settings, however, all physical needs are met. In the Benedictine monasteries, as beautifully described below, the monks had all the material resources considered necessary for intellectual and spiritual development:

> Upon entering the monastery, monks were asked to give up all of their personal possessions, conserving not even a pen or a pillow for themselves. They were also asked to surrender personal ambition and self-assertiveness, the desire to be different or to gain personal notoriety or distinction.
>
> In exchange, they received exactly what they needed to live— clothing, food, drink, writing materials, books—all in proper measure, not too much, but not too little either. Material things were given into their care but not their ownership. Because of this, each object, whether it was a chalice for the altar or a spade for the

garden, received its fitting measure of respect and attention. (Le Mée, 1994, p. 90)

Nightingale carefully studied religious orders because she felt they represented a valid attempt to organize all aspects of life, such as art, agriculture, education, etc., around a spiritual purpose. She was concerned, however, that the religious orders of her day were not making progress in understanding the laws governing spiritual development. In her view, they were more concerned with upholding dogma than in freely searching for truth (*Suggestions for Thought*, 1860/1994, pp. 141–142).

Nightingale's attitude toward religious belief is highly consistent with that of Siddhartha Gautama, known as Buddha or *the Enlightened One*. He lived in India in the 6th-century B.C., and his teachings are the foundation of Buddhism. From Buddha's perspective, blind belief is unhealthy and not conducive to spiritual development. The goal should be to attain spiritual insight so all belief is gradually transformed into knowledge and experience. Buddha admitted that some teachings had to be taken on faith in the early stages of one's spiritual development. He encouraged his students, however, to examine and question all his teachings to make sure they were consistent with what the students knew in their minds and hearts to be true.

It is not clear if Nightingale was actually influenced by Buddha, but the essence of her message reflects his advice, as quoted in a sermon:

> Do not be led by reports, or tradition, or hearsay. Be not led by the authority of religious texts, nor by mere logic or inference, nor by considering appearances, nor by the delight in speculative opinions, nor by seeming possibilities, nor by the idea: 'this is our teacher.' But . . . when you know for yourselves that certain things are unwholesome, and wrong, and bad, then give them up . . . And when you know for yourselves that certain things are wholesome and good, then accept them and follow them. (Rahula, 1959, pp. 2–3)

Nightingale was not afraid to evaluate the most comforting beliefs of religion and society because she had tremendous confidence in the benevolent design of the universe and in the human developmental process. As we reach deeper levels of insight and understanding, she felt, our beliefs will be far more health enhancing than any we have heretofore held.

REFERENCES

Barnum, B. (1996). *Spirituality in nursing: From traditional to New Age.* New York: Springer Publishing Co.

Benson, H. (1996). *Timeless healing: The power and biology of belief.* New York: Simon and Schuster.

Burkhardt, M. (1989). Spirituality: An analysis of the concept. *Holistic Nursing Practice, 3,* 69–77.

Calabria, M. (1990). Spiritual insights of Florence NIghtingale, *The Quest, 3,* 66–74.

Calabria, M., & Macrae, J. (Eds.). (1994). *Suggestions for thought by Florence Nightingale: Selections and commentaries.* Philadelphia: University of Pennsylvania Press.

Carson, V. (Ed.) (1989). *Spiritual dimensions of nursing practice.* Philadelphia: W.B. Saunders.

Cook, E. (1913). *The life of Florence Nightingale* (2 vols.) New York: Macmillan.

Dossey, B. (1999). *Florence Nightingale: Mystic, visionary, and healer.* Springhouse, PA: Springhouse.

Frankl, V. (1959). *Man's search for meaning.* New York: Simon & Schuster.

Goldie, S. (1983). *A calendar of the letters of Florence Nightingale.* Oxford: Oxford Microform Publications.

Goleman, D. (1977). *The varieties of the meditative experience.* New York: E.P. Dutton.

Le Mée, K. (1994). *Chant.* New York: Bell Tower.

Matthews, D., et al. (1993). *The faith factor: An annotated bibliography of clinical research on spiritual subjects.* Boston: John Templeton Foundation.

Miller, W. (1997). Spiritual aspects of addictions treatment and reserch. *Mind-Body Medicine, 2,* 37–43.

Moody, R. (1975). *Life after life.* New York: Bantam.

Nightingale, F. (1969). *Notes on nursing.* New York: Dover Publications. (Original work published in 1860)

O'Brien, M. E. (1999). *Spirituality in nursing: Standing on holy ground.* Sudbury, MA: Jones and Bartlett.

Rahula, W. (1959). *What the Buddha taught.* New York: Grove Press.

Richardson, R. (1986). *Henry Thoreau: A life of the mind.* Berkeley: University of California Press.

Ring, K. (1982). *Life at death: A scientific investigation of the near-death experience.* New York: Quill.

Sattin, A. (1987). *Florence Nightingale: Letters from Egypt.* New York: Weidenfeld and Nicholson.

3

Spiritual Development

Although Nightingale considered herself a Christian, that is, a follower of Christ, she did not feel that he was the only "God-man." The whole of humanity, in her view, is the incarnation of God. In *Suggestions for Thought* (1860/1994) she wrote:

> The orthodox took hold of a great truth, when they got hold of the incarnation—but they confined it to one—they did not extend it to all. . . . The true feeling of *God in us,* which led to the belief in one incarnation, ought to be extended to the incarnation *in all of us.* (pp. 14 & 15)

From Nightingale's perspective, the highest level of human consciousness is of the essence of God. It comprises all those qualities that transcend the personal ego, such as compassion, wisdom, inner peace, creativity, and the sense of the unity of life. This inner divine nature, however, must be properly nourished in order to grow and blossom:

> If our physical nature is such that, fed and exercised in one way it would be strong, healthy, efficient to perform its functions; shall we, if it is fed in a different manner, say that man's frame is by nature weak and sickly?
> We are often told that the heart of man is "desperately wicked, and deceitful above all things." Before accepting such doctrine, let us look to experience. Our feelings vary as they are exercised, as clearly as certainly as the state of the physical nature varies with its food and exercise.

If the thoughts and feelings which befit a man are called forth, a human being will be *manly* in the true sense of the word. But many hearts are turned from their natural manliness, and will be so while man's life and circumstances do not afford to his nature its proper exercise. (*Suggestions for Thought*, 1860/1994, p. 137)

Spirituality, for Nightingale, is the process of consciously cultivating the divine nature, that is, discovering and establishing the best conditions for the development of the higher qualities:

Suppose that, instead of life being regulated ignorantly, with little definite purpose, mankind, individually and collectively, aimed to organize life so as to improve character, *i.e.*, so as to extend the limits of the divine in man; can we doubt that thus man would, by exercise for himself and his kind, become more and more divine? (*Suggestions for Thought*, 1860/1994, pp. 129–30)

A Contemporary Mystical Experience

If Nightingale were alive today, she would likely be very interested in a study conducted at Oxford University in which reports of spiritual experiences were solicited from the general public. The following personal report from this study is a profound and well-articulated example of heightened spiritual awareness:

At seventeen I was confused and questing. Nothing made a lot of sense; the world seemed so unfair and people unreliable. However, I had not forgotten how to pray; and I prayed with unashamed sincerity that if God existed, could He show me some sort of light in the jungle.

One day, I was sweeping the stairs, down in the house in which I was working, when suddenly I was overcome, overwhelmed, saturated . . . with a sense of most sublime and living *love*. It not only affected me, but seemed to bring everything around me to *life*. The brush in my hand, my dustpan, the stairs, seemed to come alive with love. I seemed no longer me, with my petty troubles and trials, but part of this infinite power of love, so utterly and overwhelmingly wonderful that one knew at once what the saints had grasped. It could only have been a minute or two, yet for that brief particle of time it seemed eternity. (Cohen & Phipps, 1992, p. 67)

An experience such as this can help us gain some insight about the quality of spiritual development and the role of the spiritual dimension in health. For example, what effect might it have had on the life of the individual? Could he or she have thought, felt, and acted in the same way after such an experience? Although we cannot ask this particular person, we can find certain clues within the report itself. In the *eternal moment* reality was experienced from a different perspective. All things were brought to life by, and unified within, a divine presence characterized by love. This higher realization could have strengthened certain qualities and behaviors such as the following:

- *A sense of self-worth:* The essence of the individual was part of the divine order of love.
- *A sense of being connected to all things:* Everything, including the individual, was brought to life by the same higher power.
- *Humility:* A mundane object, such as the dustpan, was animated by the same divine love.
- *A respect for the intrinsic worth of all things:* The dustpan had a practical usefulness but, seen from this higher perspective, it was part of the divine order and thus had a value unto itself.
- *Present-centeredness:* Past and future were transcended and *for that brief particle of time it seemed eternity.*
- *Joy:* Regrets about the past and worries about the future were irrelevant, and in the eternal moment the individual felt supported by a loving and life-giving power.
- *Decreased fear of death:* The individual felt part of a timeless and transcendent order of being.

Suppose that, instead of being *confused and questing,* this individual had been ill? Could the spiritual experience have helped to alleviate some of the conditions that aggravate illness, such as loneliness, fear, anger, lack of self worth, and the inability to release negative memories? And what if this individual had been a nurse? Could the spiritual experience have helped to strengthen certain qualities that *facilitate a healing,* such as compassion, inner peace, and respect for all life?

The Cultivation of the Spirit

From Nightingale's perspective, spirituality is a developmental process that must be consciously cultivated. Nightingale felt that the society of her day was doing very little to nurture the creative vision that underlies spiritual unfolding. Organized religion, in particular, had become an arm of conventional society, bent on serving the status quo. Her particular concern was young people, whose inner divine natures were being *starved.*. She observed that many developed a spiritual vision early in life. It was not nurtured by society, however, and thus it withered and died. She wrote passionately about this in the following passage from *Suggestions for Thought* (1860/1994):

> Society triumphs over many. They wish to regenerate the world with their institutions, with their moral philosophy, with their love. . . .
> We see girls and boys of seventeen, before whose noble ambitions, heroic dreams, and rich endowments we bow our heads, as before *God incarnate in the flesh.* But, ere they are thirty, they are withered, paralyzed, extinguished. "We have forgotten our visions," they say. (pp. 97–98)

DEATH AS A STAGE OF GROWTH

Nightingale's concept of spiritual development raises an important question: What about those individuals who die young or have little opportunity to actualize their full potential? For Nightingale, the only answer that reconciles the beauty of the mystical experience with the reality of suffering and loss is the idea of life after death. If the inner spirit of humanity is of the essence of God, then it, also, should be immortal. And if spiritual development is the ultimate purpose of human life, then each individual's consciousness should be preserved so that perfect wholeness can be attained:

> Individuality appears to be sacred in the thought of God. Indeed, if we suppose man to be a modification of the attributes of God limited by the laws of physical nature, it seems natural to expect that individuality will be preserved in every instance till perfection is attained. (p. 153)

One objection to Nightingale's view can be found in the concept of succession. In this case, the ongoing spiritual development of humanity proceeds without life after death because each generation passes on its wisdom to the next, or succeeding one. The consciousness of the human race would evolve to perfection, or wholeness, but not that of each individual. Nightingale's response to this theory is based on her belief in a compassionate God:

> To suppose that each individual does contribute his portion, and then retires from existence to make room for others, is inconsistent with the hypothesis of a spirit of love and wisdom, *i.e.,* such a Being would not bring into existence a capability which, from the nature of things, no other will have, and then destroy that capability. It is true that *something* is transmitted to another generation; but experience shows that no mode of existence is wasted or destroyed. It is all evolution, development, order, progress,—never destruction. (*Suggestions for Thought,* 1860/1994, p. 148)

Although Nightingale was unclear as to the nature of the afterlife, her belief in the benevolence of God made her confident that it existed and that it provided the necessary opportunities for further growth. If we trust the kindness and consideration of our friends at the personal level, she wrote, then how much more can we trust the Eternal Divine Spirit:

> If you will strive to observe, study and comprehensively interpret the universe in its eternal purport, you will discern more and more one will, one nature, upon which you may depend. You could not bring yourself to conceive that your friends in this house would leave you this morning without your daily meal. Stretch your thought to the revelations of the universe, and still less will you feel it a possibility that God will quench the spirit than that man will starve the body. (*Suggestions for Thought,* 1860/1994, p. 154)

AN EASTERN AND A WESTERN VIEW OF SPIRITUAL DEVELOPMENT

The concept of spiritual development continuing after death is not unique to Nightingale. She studied Eastern and Western philosophical and religious traditions, and the ideas she put forth are consistent with Hindu and Platonic philosophy.

The Hindu Concept of Yoga

Nightingale became familiar with Hinduism through her friendship with Christian von Bunsen, an Egyptologist and scholar in the field of comparative religion. As a result of Bunsen's influence, translations of several Hindu texts were first published in England. Spiritual development, a fundamental concept in Hindu philosophy, is thought to unfold in a cyclic manner. Through a series of incarnations, the individual gradually achieves an integration of body and mind with the universal divine spirit. The *yogic* exercises described later in this chapter are designed to facilitate and quicken this process through conscious effort on the part of the individual.

From the Hindu perspective, the essence of the human spirit is infinite and eternal; it is identical to Brahman, the universal divine spirit. This concept is also a basic premise of Nightingale's spiritual philosophy. Huston Smith (1991), in his classic presentation of Hinduism, brings up a crucial question: If the essence of human nature is divine, why do we not act in a godlike manner? How can the Hindu hypothesis withstand the contrary evidence of the morning newspaper?

> The answer, say the Hindus, lies in the depth at which the Eternal is buried under the almost impenetrable mass of distractions, false assumptions, and self-regarding instincts that comprise our surface selves. A lamp can be covered with dust and dirt to the point of obscuring its light completely. The problem life poses for the human self is to cleanse the dross of its being to the point where its infinite center can shine forth in full display. (Smith, 1991, p. 22)

This is a very significant concept. It means that *yoga* (or any other spiritual practice) does not involve *adding* the spirit to the body and mind. Rather, it involves "cleansing the dross" of physical tensions, negative emotions, distorted thinking, etc., so that one's true creative self can emerge. We will return to this concept in subsequent chapters, because it is consistent with Nightingale's view and because many spiritual practices, including *yoga,* are based upon it.

In the Hindu tradition, *yoga* is the means through which the dross is cleansed. The term "yoga" literally means "to yoke" or "to bind." The elements that need binding or harmonizing are two different levels of human experience: the personal, in which we are conscious of separate entities existing in three-dimensional space and linear time, and the spiritual, in which all things are aspects of one unified higher reality. The meaning of *yoga* is similar to Nightingale's definition of religion as the "tie, the binding or connexion between the Perfect and the imperfect, the eternal and the temporal, the infinite and the finite, and universal and the individual."

There are *yogic* practices designed for four basic human temperaments (Smith, 1991). *Jnana yoga,* the path to unity with the divine through knowledge, is intended for those who have a strong reflective tendency. *Bhakti yoga,* the path of love, is followed by those with emotional temperaments. *Karma yoga,* designed for persons with active natures, is the path to the divine through work. *Raja yoga,* which includes physical postures and breathing exercises, is the path of psychophysical experimentation; it is intended for people who are of a scientific bent.

Raja yoga, or *8–limbed yoga,* is considered the most comprehensive system. Indeed, it is one of the most ancient holistic programs of self-integration. It was developed through centuries of experimentation and, like other systems of *yoga,* its practice requires effort and discipline on the part of the individual. Each limb of *raja yoga* is designed to "cleanse the dross" of a specific dimension of human nature.

The first two limbs, *yama* and *niyama,* reduce the anxiety that arises from unethical behavior. *Yama* means "abstinence" or "self-restraint:" it involves abstention from violence, lying, stealing, sexual misconduct, and possessiveness. *Niyama* refers to observances: the cultivation of love, contentment, purity, self-discipline, and the study of universal truths. *Asana* (physical postures) and *pranayama* (breathing exercises) help to reduce physical tension and create a rhythmic, unrestricted flow of vital energy. *Pratyahara* is the withdrawal of the mind from environmental distractions. *Dharana* (concentration) reduces the disturbances coming from internal thoughts, images, and feelings. *Dhyana* (contemplation) is the experience of inner peace and joy that arises when disturbances have been quieted. *Samadi,* the eighth limb, is an advanced phase of contemplation in which an individual's sense of separateness is transcended. The spiritual experience quoted earlier in this chapter could be considered a form of *samadi*.

Writing from the active, Western mystical perspective, Nightingale did not view spiritual experiences such as *samadi* as being the ultimate goal of human life. As she wrote in *Suggestions for Thought* (1860/1994):

> Can we suppose that God sent forth a being to suffer and struggle, merely in order that it should be re-absorbed into God's existence. Most lame and impotent conclusion. Why send it forth? To what end its suffering? (p. 153)

From Nightingale's perspective, the purpose of human existence is to implement the developmental process. Through knowledge, love, and effort, the material realm is to become a clear reflection of the divine, heavenly realm. Cleansing the dross of our personal selves allows us to become clear conduits, so to speak, for the creative energy of the divine consciousness. It allows us to fulfill our role as human beings, which is to be agents of the divine wisdom in the world, or "the working out of God's thought" (*Suggestions for Thought*, 1860/1994, p. 141).

Plato's Myth of Er

Nightingale was particularly drawn to the writings of Plato, one of the foremost Western philosophers who lived in Greece from 431–351 B.C. Plato, like Christ, utilized myths and metaphors to illustrate profound concepts. In the story of Er (*Republic*, Book 10), for example, we find the idea that the soul develops from one life to another.

The story of Er can be seen as an ancient Greek near-death experience. Er, a soldier slain in battle, came back to life after twelve days and reported his experience. According to Er's account, the quality of the afterlife experience is a direct result of the life on earth: souls were rewarded tenfold for every act of goodness they had performed and suffered tenfold for every wrong. After this period of compensation or "pilgrimage of a thousand years," every soul had to return to earth.

Er learned that every individual before birth is able to choose the type of life that will best enhance his or her development. Ideally, the character of the individual and the potential life experience should be studied and matched with great care:

> He should know what the effect of beauty is when combined with poverty or wealth in a particular soul, and what are the good and evil consequences of noble and humble birth, of private and public station, of strength and weakness, of cleverness and dullness, and of all the natural and acquired gifts of the soul, and the operation of them when conjoined; he will then look at the nature of the soul, and from the consideration of all these qualities he will be able to determine which is the better and which is the worse; and so he will choose, giving the name of evil to the life which will make his soul more unjust, and good to the life which will make his soul more just; all else he will disregard. For we have seen and know that this is the best choice both in life and after death. (Jowett, 1875/1914, pp. 412–413)

Er reported, however, that very few of the individuals he observed made the "best choice," that is, the choice that could facilitate their spiritual development. Many appeared to be influenced by a desire for prestige, wealth, or power, or by previous conditioning which limited their ability to evaluate all available options. Unfortunately, some began to regret their choices almost immediately after making them! There was no turning back, however. Everyone walked on in scorching heat through the *plain of unmindfulness* and toward evening camped by the *river of forgetfulness*. All were required to drink a certain amount from the river, but those who had not cultivated wisdom drank more than was necessary.

Theoretically, Nightingale's perspective is consistent with the myth of Er:

- Spiritual development, that is, making the soul more just, is the leading priority.

- In a lawful universe, life circumstances affect character and thus should be chosen knowledgeably and with great care.
- The afterlife is not an eternal heaven or hell, but the effects of causes generated on earth, and a new opportunity for growth.

Nightingale, like Plato, lamented the fact that many human beings, instead of evaluating and learning from life, tend to repeat the same patterns over and over again:

> Suffer as they may, they learn nothing, they would alter nothing—if they began life over again they would live exactly the same life as before. When they begin the new life in another world, they would do exactly the same thing. . . . And not only individuals, but nations learn nothing. A man once said to me, "Oh! If I were to begin again, how different I would be." But we very rarely hear this; on the contrary, we very often hear people say," I would have every moment of my life over again," and they think it pretty and grateful to God to say so. (*Suggestions for Thought,* 1860/1994, pp. 64–65)

Instead of repeating the same patterns, Nightingale felt that one should be open to change, viewing life as a noble experiment. In Er's story, for example, certain individuals acted on the belief that wealth and prestige lead to well-being. The life that followed offered an opportunity to test this belief. Ideally, the individual would evaluate the effect of wealth and prestige in "making his soul more just," and would remember this when making choices in the future. Nightingale shared Plato's optimistic view that wisdom leads to happiness both in this life and in the after-death pilgrimage of a thousand years. As he concluded the myth of Er:

> And thus . . . the tale has been saved and has not perished, and will save us if we are obedient to the word spoken; and we shall pass safely over the river of Forgetfulness and our soul will not be defiled. Wherefore my counsel is that we hold fast ever to the heavenly way and follow after justice and virtue always, considering that the soul is immortal and able to endure every sort of good and every sort of evil. Thus we shall live dear to one another and to the gods, both while remaining here and when, like the conquerors in the games

who go round to gather gifts, we receive our reward. And it shall be well with us both in this life and in the pilgrimage of a thousand years which we have been describing. (Jowett, 1875/1914, p. 397)

REFERENCES

Calabria, M. (1990). Spiritual insights of Florence Nightingale. *Quest, 3,* 66–74.

Calabria, M., & Macrae, J. (Eds.) (1994). *Suggestions for thought by Florence Nightingale: Selections and commentaries.* Philadelphia, University of Pennsylvania Press.

Cohen, J. M., & Phipps, J. F. (1992). *The common experience: Signposts on the path to enlightenment.* Wheaton, IL: Quest Books.

Cook, E. (1913). *The life of Florence Nightingale* (2 vols). New York: Macmillan.

Jowett, B. (Trans.) (1914). *The Dialogues of Plato (vol. 2).* New York: Hearsts International Library Co. (Original work published in 1875)

Newman, M. (1994). *Health as expanding consciousness.* New York: National League for Nursing Press.

Nightingale, F. (1969). *Notes on nursing.* New York: Dover Publications. (Original work published in 1860)

Ornish, D. (1998). *Love and survival.* New York: HarperCollins.

Quinn, E., & Prest, J. (Eds.). (1987). *Dear Miss Nightingale: A selection of Benjamin Jowett's letters to Florence Nightingale, 1860–1893.* Oxford: Clarendon Press.

Sattin, A. (Ed.). (1987). *Florence Nightingale, Letters from Egypt: A journey on the Nile, 1849–1850.* New York: Weidenfeld and Nicolson.

Smith, H. (1991). *The world's religions.* New York: HarperCollins.

II

Spirituality in Nursing Practice: Using the Nightingale Influence

4

Stress Reduction and Relaxation

I n *Notes on Nursing* (1860/1969), Nightingale described the external, or environmental, conditions that she felt were necessary for healing. However, she was also concerned with the internal, or psychological state of the patient and its effect on physical health. She observed that internal disturbances, such as worry and anxiety, rob the body of the energy needed for healing: "Apprehension, uncertainty, waiting, expectation, fear of surprise, do a patient more harm than any exertion" (p. 38). Today we are well aware that inner agitation, or "stress," not only interferes with the ability to heal but can also contribute to the development of illness.

Nightingale wrote emphatically that the stress level of the nurse has a profound effect on the patient: "All hurry or bustle is peculiarly painful to the sick" (*Notes on Nursing*, 1860/1969, p. 48). She emphasized the need to "possess yourself entirely," that is, to work in a steady, calm, organized manner in the sick room.

> Above all, leave the sick room quickly and come into it quickly, not suddenly, not with a rush. But don't let the patient be wearily waiting for when you will be out of the room or when you will be in it. Conciseness and decision in your movements, as well as your words, are necessarily in the sick room, as necessary as the absence of hurry and bustle. To possess yourself entirely will ensure you from either failing—either loitering or hurrying. (pp. 54–55)

As nurses, what can we do when we feel our hurry or bustle level rising? Fortunately, we have learned a great deal about stress regulation since Nightingale's time. The remainder of the chapter will be devoted to it, with particular emphasis on the work of Herbert Benson, M.D., who is investigating the relationship between spirituality and stress management through the relaxation response.

STRESS REGULATION AND HEALTH

Stress is an organism's response to life's demands. Stress can be generally defined as a state of arousal or mobilization of an organism; it is a degree of agitation that can be experienced internally and at times can be noted by an external observer of the organism (Brallier, 1982).

Hans Selye (1982), one of the earliest and foremost researchers in the field of stress regulation, emphasized the fact that stress is not intrinsically harmful. Growth and development require a certain amount of stress. It is prolonged, excessive stress that is damaging to an organism:

> Stress is the spice of life when it motivates us to achieve more; this is "eustress," which is good for us. Stress can also defeat us and cause "distress" when we are overcome by it. If distress lasts long enough, it will lead to tissue breakdown in the body or to mental disturbance. Eventually, it will cause such stress-related diseases as high blood pressure, cardiovascular disease, ulcers, asthma, allergies, and many other psychosomatic illnesses. . . .
>
> Successful stress management finds ways of increasing resistance to stress and reducing its harmful effects. It is also a valuable type of preventive medicine. The inability to cope with stress is the most important issue facing us; hence, managing stress is the answer to most of our health problems and the road to happiness. Indulgence in short term stress reducers such as smoking, drinking coffee, tea, or alcohol, taking drugs, etc. seems to help us initially, but we soon need ever increasing amounts to get the same effect. Also, these alternatives are all addictive and become problems in themselves. A better method of stress reduction would be relaxation, which involves changes in our attitudes, behaviors, and lifestyles.
>
> Stress management entails a balanced diet in quantities that will ensure optimum weight and nutrition, routine daily exercise, suffi-

cient sleep to let the body rest and heal itself, and relaxation techniques. (pp. vi-vii)

The regulation of stress can be found in the spiritual practices of both Eastern and Western cultures. *Ashtanga, or 8-limbed yoga,* described in chapter 3, is a fine example. Yoga is designed to yoke the personal self with the inner spirit, creating a state of wholeness. From the yogic perspective, the tensions and disturbances within the mind and body cloud over, so to speak, the clear sky of the spirit (Taimni, 1961). The eightfold system (ethics, breathing exercises, physical postures, meditation, etc.) was designed to eliminate these disturbances and heal the fragmentation. We could thus view *Ashtanga yoga* as one of the first holistic stress management programs in human history.

In the medieval Christian monastic tradition, we find that life was organized in such a way as to prevent excessive agitation. In monastic life, periods of quietude were an integral part of the daily schedule. Time was allotted for participation in services, meditation, and prayer. Even meals were taken in silence. These periods of quietude, scheduled at regular intervals, gave life a rhythm: periods of moderate stress alternating with periods of low stress in which accumulated tension can be released.

In modern secular society (including the health care facilities), the pace of life is faster and more hectic than that of the monasteries, so the stress level is more intense. It is difficult to find a quiet place or time to release accumulated tension. In addition, periods of quietude are not formally included in most work schedules. Thus the physical, mental, and spiritual problems associated with prolonged, excessive stress are more likely to arise. The challenge in modern life is for each individual to create a lifestyle in which periods of activity and periods of quietude are integrated.

EVOKING THE RELAXATION RESPONSE

Health problems associated with the high stress levels of modern society have sparked renewed interest in meditation, imagery, yoga, and other therapies that promote relaxation (Brallier, 1982; Dossey et al., 2000; Goleman & Gurin, 1993). Dr. Herbert Benson, a well-known researcher in the field of mind/body medicine, coined the term *relaxation response*. In his words, this response:

> Refers to the inborn capacity of the body to enter a special state characterized by lowered heart rate, decreased rate of breathing, lowered blood pressure, slower brain waves, and an overall reduction in the speed of metabolism. . . . The changes produced by this Response counteract the harmful effects and uncomfortable feelings of stress. (Benson, 1984, p. 4)

Benson's Method

After reviewing both Eastern and Western practices that lead to the relaxation response, Benson (1975) identified four basic components: a quiet environment; a comfortable position; a mental device such as a sound, word, or image upon which to focus the mind; and, most important, a passive attitude (pp. 158–160). The following is a method that Benson practices himself and also uses in his clinical practice and research:

1. Pick a focus word or short phrase that's firmly rooted in your belief system.
2. Sit quietly in a comfortable position.
3. Close your eyes.
4. Relax your muscles.
5. Breathe slowly and naturally, and as you do, repeat your focus word, phrase or short prayer silently to yourself as you exhale.
6. Assume a passive attitude. Don't worry about how well you're doing. When other thoughts come to mind, simply say to yourself, "Oh well," and gently return to the repetition.
7. Continue for ten to twenty minutes.
8. Do not stand immediately. Continue sitting quietly for a minute or so, allowing other thoughts to return. Then open your eyes and sit for another minute before rising.
9. Practice this technique once or twice daily (Benson, 1996, p. 136).

This method can be viewed from different perspectives, depending on one's philosophic or religious orientation and underlying intent. For example, it can be used as a relaxation technique, as a form of contemplative prayer, or as a concentrative meditation exercise.

BENSON'S METHOD AS A RELAXATION EXERCISE

The technique is based on the long-held belief that a calm, focused mind is associated with a relaxed body, while a noisy, scattered mind is associated with physical tension. During the first practice session, you will probably notice some physiological signs of relaxation, such as a slower and deeper breathing pattern, a loosening of your muscles, a slower heart rate, etc. As a relaxation exercise, any mental focus can be effective. If you cannot find a word or phrase that suits you, pick a sound or an image. You might also try focusing on a symbol of life's movement, such as the sound of the wind or a flowing stream. The rhythm of your breathing or heartbeat can also be a helpful relaxation focus. Allow yourself to become one with the rhythm. Feel the fluidity of your body processes at work. If your jaw, chest, stomach, or another area feels tight and constricted, imagine the tension melting away as sunlight melts a block of ice. You can also try a *yogic* technique of breathing into the tight area: feel your breath penetrate and dissolve the tension, and let the tension flow out with the release of your breath.

A relaxation exercise such as this can also have profound psychological benefits. For example, Benson writes that in his clinical experience evoking the relaxation response helps a person break free of restrictive "worry cycles:"

> In this relatively peaceful condition, the individual's mental patterns change so that he breaks free of what I call "worry cycles." These are unproductive grooves or circuits that cause the mind to "play" over and over again, almost involuntarily, the same anxieties or uncreative, health-impairing thoughts. (Benson, 1984, pp. 4–5)

This type of exercise supports the development of spirituality by creating a state of inner quietude that is receptive to more subtle, creative, and expansive levels of awareness. From Nightingale's perspective, our habitual thinking processes block the creative vision of the inner divine nature. As our minds become quieter, therefore, we can begin to experience the clarity and peace that is always within us.

BENSON'S EXERCISE AND CENTERING PRAYER

Benson's technique is very similar to the centering prayer exercise discussed in chapter 7. Keating (1992) writes that centering prayer is associated with physical relaxation. The physical response would appear to be a side effect, however, as the basic intent or motivation is to attune to the inner presence of God.

Interestingly, Benson (1984; 1996) has found that a religious focus enhances the relaxation response. His explanation is that the religious beliefs associated with the focus enhance the power of the placebo effect (that is, the positive influence of belief on the body) and this increases the level of physical relaxation. He also observes that people who choose a focus that draws upon their deepest philosophic or religious convictions are more likely to practice regularly, thus enhancing the benefits of the exercise.

BENSON'S EXERCISE AND CONCENTRATIVE MEDITATION

Meditation practices can be divided into two broad categories: *concentrative* and *insight* (Goleman, 1977). During concentrative meditation the individual learns to still the mind by holding his or her attention on one specific object or process, such as a sound, an image, or the rhythm of the breath. During insight meditation (see chapter 6) the individual observes, in a nonattached manner, all the physical sensations, emotions, and thoughts that come into awareness.

The method that we have been discussing is similar to concentrative meditation because it involves focusing the mind on a word or phrase. Concentrative meditation is based on the theory that a quiet mind *both* relaxes the body and attunes to the spirit. The underlying intent is to quiet mind and body in order to connect with deeper levels of being from which arise peace, wisdom, and compassion.

The fact that both concentrative meditation and contemplative prayer are associated with relaxation supports the idea that body and spirit are connected, and thus that which nourishes one will also nourish the other.

Common Questions about the Relaxation Response

For beginners, the regular practice of a relaxation method generally brings up some questions. The issues that follow are representative of these concerns:

- "How often do I have to practice?"

Relaxation is a skill that must be developed with regular practice. In a fast-paced society relaxing does not come naturally. You can sit in front of the television at night harboring the same physical stress level that plagued you all day at work. Therefore, to be deeply beneficial, the relaxation exercise needs to be woven into the daily pattern of your life.

In a monastic setting one can effortlessly follow a preplanned schedule that includes meditation periods. In secular society, however, we have to place a high value on inner quietude and make a determined effort to integrate relaxation into our daily schedule.

You may find that a particular time is most conducive for meditation. Many feel that practicing in the morning helps them begin the day with a relaxed and positive attitude. Practicing at lunchtime helps prevent an escalation of tension during the day, particularly if you are able to leave the clinical area and sit in a peaceful place, such as a chapel or garden. For many, the best time for practice is in the evening since the relaxation exercise helps us not only to release accumulated tension, but also to assimilate the experiences of the day. Practicing at bedtime helps some people sleep better. For others, however, it has a refreshing and energizing effect and thus it keeps them awake!

Practice whenever it is most comfortable for you, even if it is different from one day to the next. The number of minutes you spend on the exercise is less important than the regularity and sincerity of your practice. Although 20 minutes is generally recommended, give yourself the time that you need, which may also vary from day to day. A relaxation technique should not be considered a duty, artificially imposed on a crowded schedule, but an integrating process that we enjoy and that gives an inner balance to our outward lives.

• "I often feel so wound up that I cannot sit down and do the exercise."

If you feel too wound up to focus, some preliminary steps can be helpful, such as taking a brisk walk around the block or listening to relaxing music. You could also do some stretching exercises or simply rub some of the tension out of your shoulders, hands, and feet. If you are hungry, you should eat something so as not to be disturbed by pangs in your stomach. Consider a small snack, since the digesting of a heavy meal can interfere with your ability to focus. Try to remove potential distractions beforehand. For example, if you have a phone call to make, do it first, if possible, so you will not worry about it during the exercise.

The fact remains, however, that on some days it is easier to relax than on others. Life changes from day to day, not only our external conditions but our internal states as well. Thus our practice is never twice the same. Sometimes we respond to a relaxation session emotionally more than physically, sometimes a valuable insight arises, sometimes it appears as if nothing happens. So the best advice is this: Let go of memories and expectations and approach each experience with a fresh, open mind.

• "I start the exercise and immediately fall asleep."

Falling asleep during the exercise simply means that you are tired! Many of us begin to learn stress regulation with an accumulation of repressed fatigue, and the relaxation process brings us in touch with it. In Nightingale's view, this underlying fatigue is dangerous because it can damage our health. There is a wisdom within the body, a tendency towards order and balance, but without adequate energy it cannot be maximized.

Although a relaxation technique does not take the place of adequate sleep and rest, it does helps to reenergize both the mind and the body. Because of this, the tendency to fall asleep during the exercise generally won't last for more than a week or two. We are somewhat conditioned to fall asleep when our bodies relax, because we enter a relaxed state at the beginning of our nightly sleep cycle. It is best not to lie down during your practice session, therefore, but to sit comfortably erect on a chair or cushion. This position will help you recondition yourself to enter a relaxed state while maintaining your conscious awareness.

Nursing students, in particular, are sometimes disappointed to learn that the regular practice of a relaxation technique does not eliminate the need for sleep. They seem to regard sleep as an unwelcome intruder who robs them of precious hours every night. It is true that the regular practice of relaxation may reduce the need for sleep by helping to alleviate stress-related fatigue. It does not eliminate the need for sleep, however. Research studies have demonstrated that subjects in highly controlled, low-stress environments still have to sleep (Dement, 1976).

It would appear that physical rest is only one function of the mysterious process of sleep. Indeed, EEG studies have revealed that sleep is not an inert state but a state of intense inner activity. Remember that the human organism is part of nature, and nature's activity is organized in rhythms and cycles. If we look at some of the most obvious rhythms, such as the heartbeat or the movement of the tides, we notice a period of expansion followed by a period of contraction. It is reasonable to suppose that human consciousness follows this same pattern: a period of outward activity followed by a period of inner activity. If we resist this basic pattern, we create friction between ourselves and nature—which we feel as fatigue.

- "I sometimes get a headache or feel lightheaded."

Headaches often arise from shoulder and neck tension. Before you start your exercise, therefore, it is helpful to rub your shoulders and gently rotate your neck to relieve some of the tension and reduce the likelihood of a headache. Headaches can also arise if you try too hard, if you try to force your mind to stay focused. You should train your mind with a "firm gentleness," the way you might train a pet whom you love. Remember that you do not have to perform the exercise perfectly or grade yourself after each session. The results are cumulative, and it is the sincerity and regularity of your practice that matters.

Lightheadedness or a "floating" feeling often comes from tension in the legs and feet. Lack of circulation in the lower extremities reduces our energy exchange with the earth, giving us an *ungrounded* feeling. If this happens, stop the exercise for a few minutes and give yourself a foot massage. When you return to the relaxation exercise, you might focus on an image of a healthy tree with strong, deep roots. Think of *yourself* as that tree and feel your connection with the earth.

* "I get distracted by physical sensations such as muscle twitching and rumbling in my stomach."

Practicing a relaxation exercise helps us to release the tension that obstructs communication with our deeper nature. This is generally a gradual process, the tension being peeled off in layers, so to speak. It accounts for many of the unusual sensations we sometimes experience, such as muscle twitching, migratory pains, shivering spells, and heaviness in the hands and feet. Stomach rumbling and flushing of the skin (vasodilation of the peripheral blood vessels) are due to parasympathetic nervous system activity, a normal part of the relaxation response. Generally, these sensations are transitory. If they are particularly bothersome, or if they "spill over" into the rest of your day, it is helpful to reduce the number of minutes you spend practicing the exercise (Carrington, 1987).

Remember that there is a wisdom within the body, a tendency towards order and balance. Nightingale (1860/1969) was aware of this when she wrote that "Nature alone cures . . . and what nursing has to do . . . is to put the patient in the best condition for nature to act upon him" (p. 133). When we practice relaxation, we put ourselves in an appropriate condition for healing and Nature begins to work!

* "When I look inward I see so much negativity that I stop the exercise."

The healing process helps to release emotional as well as physical tension. Our unexpressed *negative* feelings such as anger, frustration, guilt, sadness, etc., are often pushed down, so to speak, below the level of our normal awareness. When we practice relaxation, our awareness deepens and we may occasionally experience waves of emotion. The best approach—one that is recommended by most stress management and meditation instructors—is to acknowledge these feelings and return to the focus of the exercise. It is often helpful to look at them as clouds that will eventually drift away and reveal the clear sky behind them. If a specific feeling keeps recurring in meditation, however, or if it starts emerging into your dreams or working hours, you might discuss this with a therapist or knowledgeable friend. This could help you gain insight and quicken the release of the tension.

Some thoughts and feelings that we regard as negative and tend to repress are not meant to be released but acknowledged and integrated. In Jungian dreamwork (Von Franz, 1964) these are represented by the "shadow," a figure of the same sex as the dreamer who appears and/or acts in a way that the dreamer finds personally unacceptable. For example, as nurses we like to feel that we are always knowledgeable, compassionate, well-organized, and able to handle a demanding workload. Thus our shadow might represent our repressed desire for solitude, for questioning and doubt, and for relaxation and play. If we do not acknowledge these needs, we fragment ourselves and waste a great deal of energy. Part of the healing process—which relaxation facilitates—is to bring the shadow into the light of consciousness and to integrate it positively and creatively.

- "What can I do if I am feeling tense or tired or irritable in the clinical area?"

Dora Kunz (1986), a well-known healer, recommended that nurses perform very short meditation and relaxation exercises during their clinical day. For example, in the half minute you take to wash your hands between patients, you could:

1. Take a deep breath;
2. Quiet your mind using your mental focus; and
3. Think of the tension flowing out of you and going down the drain.

The importance of short exercises such as this cannot be overestimated. They are an important step in learning to "possess yourself entirely," that is, to maintain a calm presence in the midst of stressful external circumstances. As Nightingale (1860/1969) wrote, "All hurry or bustle is peculiarly painful to the sick" (p. 48). Relaxation, therefore, not only helps to enhance our own well-being, but also to maintain excellence in patient care. The short exercises, however useful, should be an *extension* of your regular practice, not a substitute for it. Practicing regularly in a conducive environment helps to improve your baseline level of relaxation, making the short exercises much more effective.

Relaxation and Time Experience

One of the most common reports from individuals who learn a relaxation method is a change in the subjective experience of time. To our ordinary waking consciousness time flows in a linear stream from the past into the future. For many individuals, this flow is far too fast: work, school, and family responsibilities all seem to be fulfilled in a race with time. The health care system is no exception. Hospital nursing practice is particularly embedded in linear time with treatments, meals, medications, end of shift reports, and so on, being strictly regulated by the clock. All too often, high-quality care must be squeezed into rapidly vanishing moments.

Physician Larry Dossey (1981) writes that the feeling of being trapped in linear time is the cause of many current health problems:

> Our sense of urgency results in a speeding of some of our body's rhythmical functions, such as the heart rate and respiratory rate. Exaggerated rises in the blood pressure may follow, along with increases in blood levels of specific hormones that are involved in the body's response to stress. Thus, our perceptions of speeding clocks and vanishing time cause our own biological clocks to speed. . . . The end result is frequently some form of "hurry sickness" expressed as heart disease, high blood pressure, or depression of our immune function, leading to an increased susceptibility to infection and cancer. (p. 49)

Hurry sickness can be cured, Dossey explains, by learning to experience time in a nonlinear manner. Interestingly, there is no "objective" manner of time experience. Although a clock ticks regularly, human beings subjectively experience time irregularly. When we are engaged in an interesting or enjoyable activity, time flows quickly and lightly; when we are engaged in an activity that is neither interesting nor enjoyable, time flows slowly and heavily. Sometimes, when we are completely absorbed in an activity, time seems to stand still.

Nonlinear time can be experienced whenever our minds are completely focused on what we are doing. The relaxation exercise described above or any of the spiritual practices presented in this book can give us the experience of nonlinear time. In a study of meditation (Macrae, 1982), nonlinear time was measured with the Time Metaphor Test, an instrument constructed with metaphors from world literature that described the passing of time. Experienced meditators were asked to perform a 20-minute exercise (using whatever technique they preferred) and afterward to choose 5 metaphors on the test that best described their experience of time during the meditation session. A control group, composed of subjects who did not practice meditation, was asked to sit quietly for 20 minutes and afterward to choose 5 metaphors that best described the experience of time during the quiet period.

The results revealed a significant difference in time experience between meditating and nonmeditating subjects. Meditating subjects tended to choose nonlinear metaphors, such as "a quiet, motionless ocean" or "a vast expanse of sky." Nonmeditators tended to choose linear metaphors for the passing of time, such as "a speeding train" or "an arrow in flight." It is interesting that not one of the forty-five meditating subjects chose "a tedious song," which might indicate boredom, and only two chose "the Rock of Gibraltar," which might indicate heaviness. In addition, almost half the sample of meditators chose the metaphor "budding leaves" which suggests the qualities of freshness, hopefulness, and growth.

Learning to "step outside" of linear time on a regular basis yields some important benefits:

1. *Improved physical health.* A break from the pressures of linear time gives the body a chance to recuperate from "hurry sickness" and return to its normal rhythmical functioning.

2. *Clearer priorities*. We must accept the fact that linear time is limited. We cannot take advantage of every opportunity that is offered. Frequently we cannot do everything we would like to for each patient. We have to choose, and choose wisely. Entering non-linear time gives us a vantage point from which to reevaluate priorities so the linear flow of time can be utilized more effectively.

3. *A greater sense of joy*. If we live only in linear time, the present can become tainted with worries about the future or with regrets and resentments from the past. The regular practice of meditation and other spiritual disciplines helps us access the dimension of our consciousness that transcends these negative elements. In the "eternal moment" regrets and worries lose their power. Nonlinear time experience thus helps us to live more fully in the present moment and enjoy the flow of our lives.

Teaching Relaxation to Patients

Illness, particularly when it requires hospitalization, is a great source of stress. And stress, as Nightingale (1860/1969) observed, "does the patient more harm than any exertion" (p. 38). When you feel comfortable using a relaxation exercise such as that described above, you could begin sharing it with your patients. They can be taught to use the exercise once or twice a day for general relaxation; before an anxiety-producing diagnostic test or procedure; or after a procedure to help release tension and promote rest and recovery. The following are some general guidelines for helping patients to evoke the relaxation response. The guidelines are also appropriate for the spiritual exercises and methods discussed in subsequent chapters:

• Make sure you are relaxed when you teach the exercise. Remember that patients respond to your presence as well as to your words and deeds. A calm presence will help the patient relax.

• Determine whether or not the patient is interested in the exercise and if he or she has the strength to focus his or her mind for a short period. If the patient is unable to focus, a relaxation tape or soothing music (of the patient's choice) might be helpful.

• Allow the patient to choose his or her own meaningful focus for the exercise. If the patient seems hesitant about choosing one, you could assist by making some suggestions.

• Try to stay and support the patient the first time he or she does the exercise. Relaxation, prayer, and meditation are often more effective when performed in a group setting. There appears to be a synergistic effect when people engage in the practice together and support one another. If you can, try to do the exercise *with* the patient.

• Evaluate the patient's response. People are sometimes hesitant about describing their internal responses. Gently encourage feedback so you can offer further assistance.

• As repressed material can sometimes arise as the patient relaxes more deeply, recommend available resources (therapists, organizations, books, etc.) that could provide help if needed.

REFERENCES

Benson, H. (1975). *The relaxation response.* New York: Avon Books.

Benson, H. (1984). *Beyond the relaxation response.* New York: Times Books.

Benson, H. (1996). *Timeless healing: The power and biology of belief.* New York: Simon and Schuster.

Brallier, L. (1982). *Successfully managing stress.* Los Altos, CA: National Nursing Review.

Calabria, M., & Macrae, J. (Eds.). (1994). *Suggestions for thought by Florence Nightingale: Selections and commentaries.* Philadelphia: University of Pennsylvania Press.

Carrington, P. (1987). *Freedom in meditation* (3rd ed.). Kendall Park, NJ: Pace Educational Systems.

Dement, W. (1976). *Some must watch while some must sleep.* New York: W.W. Norton.

Dossey, L. (1982). *Space, time and medicine.* Boulder: Shambhala.

Dossey, B., Keegan, L., & Guzzetta, C. (Eds.). (2000). *Holistic nursing: A handbook for practice.* Gaithersburg, MD: Aspen Publications.

Goleman, D. (1977). *The varieties of the meditative experience.* New York: E.P. Dutton.

Goleman, D., & Gurin, J. (Eds.). (1993). *Mind/body medicine.* Yonkers, NY: Consumer Reports Books.

Keating, T. (1992). *Open mind, open heart: The contemplative dimension of the Gospel.* New York: Continuum.

Kunz, D. (1986). *Lecture notes.* Craryville, NY: Pumpkin Hollow Farm.

Macrae, J. (1982). *A comparison between meditating subjects and non-meditating subjects on time experience and human field motion.* Unpublished Doctoral Dissertation, New York University.

Nightingale, F. (1873). A sub-'note' of interrogation. *Fraser's Magazine,* 88, 25–36.

Nightingale, F. (1969). *Notes on nursing.* New York: Dover Publications. (Original work published in 1860)

Quinn, J. (1992). Holding sacred space: The nurse as healing environment. *Holistic Nursing Practice, 6,* 26–36.

Selye, H. (1982). Forward. In L. Brallier, *Successfully managing stress.* Los Altos, CA: National Nursing Review.

Smith, H. (1991). *The world's religions.* New York: HarperCollins.

Taimni, I. K. (1961). *The science of yoga.* Wheaton, IL: Theosophical Publishing House.

Von Franz, M. L. (1964). The process of individuation. In C. Jung, et al. (Eds.), *Man and his symbols.* Garden City, NY: Doubleday and Company.

5

Compassion

Nightingale's study of mystical experiences convinced her of the transcendent unity of all things in God. From her perspective, closeness to God is the wellspring of compassion. In the following passage from *Suggestions for Thought* (1860/ 1994), she explains that time spent alone, in union with God, must also bring us closer to humanity, whose inner essence is divine:

> It is said that mysticism is mistaken in urging man to isolate himself with God, and devote himself exclusively to his Creator; whereas man's natural inclination, implanted in him by God, urges him to devote himself to his fellow man, urges all mankind mutually to unite in benevolent ties. But those who say this do not see that the first motive for mankind is to unite in devotion to God, that devotion to God is the spring of love to man, makes it necessary, is the same thing. One with God, one with man. (p. 129)

From Nightingale's perspective, compassion or universal love arises from the inner God-consciousness. As the personal self becomes unified with the spirit through the process of evolution, higher qualities such as compassion become actualized. Her view is consistent with the world's religions. Great figures such as Christ and Buddha have exemplified the compassionate life. In the *Bhagavad Gita,* the sacred Hindu poem, compassion is one of the characteristics of the spiritually realized individual:

> Fearlessness, singleness of soul, the will
> Always to strive for wisdom; opened hand

And governed appetites; and piety
And love of lonely study; humbleness;
Uprightness, heed to injure nought which lives,
Truthfulness, slowness unto wrath, a mind
That lightly letteth go what others prize;
And equanimity, and charity
Which spieth no man's faults; and tenderness
Towards all that suffer. (Arnold, 1975, p. 129)

COMPASSION AND UNITY

The ultimate unity of life, discovered by both mystics and scientists, lies at the foundation of compassion. The word compassion comes from the Latin *compassio,* which means "to feel with." It can be seen as a form of spiritual or universal love that embraces all individuals regardless of personal attributes.

The following personal report, another from the Oxford University study of spontaneous spiritual experiences mentioned in chapter 3, contains a description of compassion as a spiritual quality. In this individual's experience, compassion lay beyond the likes and dislikes of the personal, emotional realm and was extended to "all people on earth."

Although religion had meant a lot to me, at the same time I was going through a period of doubt and disillusion with life and was torn by conflict . . . On this particular June day I had time to fill in. It was a glorious sunny evening and I walked through St. James Park and sat down by the water intending to read. I never opened my book.

It was very beautiful, with the sun glinting through the trees and the ducks swimming on the water, and quite suddenly I felt lifted beyond all the turmoil and the conflict. There was no visual imagery and I knew I was sitting on a seat in the park, but I felt as if I was lifted above the world and looking down on it. The disillusion and cynicism were gone and I felt compassion suffusing my whole being, compassion for all people on earth. I was possessed by a peace that I have never felt before or since and—what is to me most interesting and curious of all—this whole state was not emotional; it was as if

I was not without emotion but beyond it. The experience passed off gradually and I suppose it lasted twenty to thirty minutes. At the time I felt it was an experience of God, because I interpreted it according to my own religious framework. (Cohen & Phipps, 1992, pp. 67–68)

Huxley (1945), in his cross-cultural study of mystical experiences, identified three components of universal love, or charity, as he called it: disinterestedness, tranquility, and humility. In the experience quoted above we find disinterestedness because the individual had transcended the realm of personal emotion. There was neither a desire for personal gain, nor any fear of loss, only a universal love for humanity.

There was also tranquility because the experience was associated with "a peace that I have never felt before or since." This striking statement supports the mystical view that conflict and anxiety exist only at the personal or material level of reality. Our sense of personal separateness can, unfortunately, engender feelings of loneliness, uncertainty, inadequacy, vulnerability, etc. At the spiritual level, however, all is unified; personal separateness does not exist so anxiety is not aroused. From the mystical perspective, therefore, the underlying purpose of evoking the relaxation response is to quiet mind and body so that one's consciousness can be touched by the peace of the inner spirit.

Nightingale's study of science reinforced the concept of the ultimate unity of life which is found in the mystical traditions. Her work in statistics, in particular, revealed hidden connections among phenomena which, on the surface, appeared to be separate. She felt statistics was a sacred science because it allowed one to transcend one's limited personal perspective and read the thoughts of God.

If Nightingale were alive today, she would be interested in the discoveries of modern physics. It has been found that the smallest particles of matter, within the nucleus of the atom, are not solid, separate entities. Fritjof Capra, in his classic book *The Tao of Physics* (1975), wrote that the subatomic world is dynamic and unified:

All particles can be transmuted into other particles; they can be created from energy and vanish into energy. In this world, classical concepts like 'elementary particle,' 'material substance,' or 'isolated object,' have lost their meaning: the whole universe appears as a dynamic web of inseparable energy patterns. (p. 80)

Capra (1975), discussing the similarities between the worldview of modern physics and that of the Eastern mystical traditions, comes to a conclusion that is consistent with Nightingale's vision over 100 years before:

Eastern thought and, more generally, mystical thought, provide a consistent and relevant philosophical background to the theories of contemporary science; a conception of the world in which man's scientific discoveries can be in perfect harmony with his spiritual aims and religious beliefs. (p. 25)

THE LOVING-KINDNESS MEDITATION

Compassion, like all spiritual qualities, can be consciously cultivated. Indeed, as compassion is integral to the divine consciousness, any exercise that helps to integrate body and mind with the inner spirit will help to deepen our experience of compassion. The following is a traditional Buddhist meditation that is specifically designed to help us gradually broaden our perspective, from the level of personal love to the level universal love. This meditation allows us to experience the fact that "nonpersonal" does not mean "noncaring;" it means a level of caring that is equally available to all.

There are many versions of the loving-kindness meditation. Below, it is described by Ayya Khema (1991) during a retreat with students.

First, concentrate on the breath for just a minute.

Let compassion arise in your heart for yourself and for all the *dukkha* [that is, anxiety, pain, difficulties, lack of fulfillment, dissatisfaction, etc.] that has already happened in this life, is there now, and may yet come. Compassion for the lack of realization and compassion for the difficulties of the practice. Let this feeling embrace you and hold you safe and secure.

Extend the compassion from your heart to the person sitting nearest you; compassion for all the *dukkha* in his or her life that has been, is now and may yet come, compassion for the difficulties arising in meditation. Embracing the person, holding him or her tight, giving him or her a sense of being cared for.

Extend your compassion to everyone meditating with you, remembering that everyone has *dukkha*. Remembering that everyone would like care and concern, embracing everyone with your compassion.

Think of your parents. Let the compassion for their difficulties and their *dukkha* arise in your heart. Embrace them, showing them your care and concern.

Think of those people nearest and dearest to you. Have compassion for their *dukkha,* their difficulties, their pain. Embrace them with your love and compassion, showing them your care and concern.

Think of all your friends, let compassion arise in your heart, let them know you care, that you feel with them. Embrace them with that feeling.

Think of anyone whom you find difficult to love and think of that person with a feeling of compassion arising in you. Compassion for that person's *dukkha* and difficulties, lack of both freedom and liberation. Let this compassion really reach out to that person, filling him or her and surrounding him or her with it.

Think of all those people whose lives are far more difficult than ours. They may be in hospitals, in prisons, in refugee camps, in war-torn countries; they may be hungry, crippled, blind, without shelter or friends. Let this heart of compassion reach out to all of them, embracing them with it, feeling with them, realizing their pain, wishing to help.

Move your attention back to yourself and let this feeling of compassion fill you from head to toe and surround you, giving you a sense of being helped and cared for, accepted, at ease.

May all beings have compassion for each other. (pp. 28–30)

The critical point in this exercise is the short period of transition from your friends to the person you find difficult to love. When you can keep the same expansive feeling of loving kindness during this shift of focus, you have touched upon a higher, nonpersonal level of love.

UNITY AND INDIVIDUALITY

In *Suggestions for Thought* (1860/1994) Nightingale wrote that "individuality appears to be sacred in the thought of God" (p. 153). She felt that the entire evolutionary process was designed to create wholeness through the integration of body, mind, and spirit. And yet the experience of spirituality appears to bring about a loss of personal separateness; one feels part of a larger whole. Addressing the paradox of individuality and universality, Owens (1972) wrote that our individuality is supported and strengthened by the sense of being rooted in a universal source of peace, order, and beauty:

> The universality which the mystic experiences may temporarily result in a loss of personal identity; afterward, there is a deepening of the perception of self in the knowledge that all selves are one. Thoreau, for example, lived alone in the woods for two years, losing himself in participation in something much larger than his own personality. The result was an intensely personal yet universal statement, *Walden,* which has been a source of strength to readers because it rings so true, without a false note. He who can truly participate in nature, or fuse with the universality of life, touches a source of serenity, order, beauty and harmony which breathes through all his days. The lives of Lao-Tsu, Socrates, Ramakrishna bear witness. (pp. 149–150)

Compassion and Overidentification

As compassion, or universal love, arises from a spiritual source, it should never diminish our sense of wholeness or personal integrity. Unfortunately, in nursing practice, compassion is sometimes confused with a sympathetic overidentification with the patient's suffering. To better understand the relationship between compassion and personal identification, it is helpful to examine two behavioral modes identified by Quinn (1981) and the way in which these modes can be transcended.

In the *sympathetic mode,* the needfulness of the patient triggers a sympathetic response in the nurse. He or she identifies with the patient and feels as the patient does. The patient's hopes and fears all become the nurse's. The feelings of the patient remain with the nurse, even while at home in the evening and on his or her days off.

This mode creates obvious problems for both the nurse and the patient. The nurse becomes fatigued because he or she not only absorbs a great deal of negatively charged energy from the patient, but also pours out a great deal of personal energy. And when the nurse becomes tired from overidentifying in this way, the patient is less likely to receive an accurate assessment, peaceful support, or other elements of high-quality care.

The *defensive mode* is the opposite of the sympathetic mode. Here the needfulness and demands of the patient arouse anxiety in the nurse, and he or she unconsciously utilizes a variety of self-protective behaviors. These behaviors may include emotional distancing and withdrawal; excessive task-orientedness; derogatory labeling of the patient as "demanding" or 'uncooperative;' inappropriate levity and jocularity; false reassurance; or becoming angry with the patient in order to justify the avoidance.

This mode also creates problems for both the nurse and the patient. The nurse becomes fatigued because it takes energy to develop and maintain a personal defense mechanism. Feelings of guilt can arise within the nurse, because he or she is acting in a way that is not consistent with the image of a nurse as a caring professional. In this mode, as in the sympathetic mode, the patient is deprived of a supportive relationship.

Quinn (personal communication, August 14, 1982) observes that although some nurses tend to utilize one of these modes, others seem unconsciously to vacillate between the two. Thus we see an interplay of opposites which can be transcended through the *holistic mode*.

The *holistic mode* is the mode of compassion. As Quinn (1991) describes, the nurse in this mode acts in a highly conscious manner. He or she is aware of the patient's state of being and of his or her personal response. Therefore, any desire to overidentify or withdraw is recognized. The holistic mode allows the nurse to relax, to think of him or herself as an open system of energy, and to draw on vital energies in the environment, so that as energy is given out, it is immediately replenished. In the holistic mode, "the outflow of the nurse's energies becomes a conscious, focused, and regulated process, in contrast with the automatic, unconscious, and unregulated reactions that characterize the defensive mode and the sympathetic mode" (p. 208).

Compassion and the Holistic Mode

From Nightingale's perspective, it is through the development of spirituality that the holistic mode can be most fully utilized. The integration of body, mind, and spirit brings a sense of intrinsic wholeness or completeness within oneself. When we have a secure sense of our own identity, the needfulness that triggers the sympathetic mode and the vulnerability that triggers the defensive mode are both diminished. And when personal needs fade into the background, we can more fully act in the best interests of another.

The development of spirituality also enhances the conscious regulation of energy mentioned above, because it allows us to access the unlimited compassionate energy of the spiritual dimension. Dr. Joan Borysenko (1998) one of the leading proponents of mind/body medicine, writes that compassion enhances the vitality of both giver and receiver:

> What I think is going on from a mystical point of view is that we are all systems of energy interconnected with all other energies. . . . If we open our hearts, the energy simply flows in and we are nourished by it. It flows in. And not only that, but it also flows out. An interesting piece of preliminary research about that is a pilot study that Dr. Janet Quinn did on therapeutic touch. She was measuring an index of immune function in people getting therapeutic touch, where the practitioner becomes a channel for life-force energy. This energy flows when the practitioner's heart is opened by feeling great respect, love, and care for the person he or she is helping. Dr. Quinn found that immune function increased in the person getting therapeutic touch, but it increased just as much in the person giving it. When the heart is open, that life-force energy doesn't end with us. An open-hearted person is always giving to someone else, and the act of giving is simultaneously the act of receiving. (pp. 192–193)

The simultaneity of giving and receiving in an act of compassion is poetically described by Shakespeare in these famous lines from *The Merchant of Venice:*

> The quality of mercy is not strain'd
> It droppeth as the gentle rain from heaven

Upon the place beneath: it is twice bless'd;
It blesseth him that gives and him that takes.

Implementing the Holistic Mode

The following exercise can help you actualize the concept of an energy "flow-through" described in the previous section. It is adapted from a series of exercises developed by Kunz and Peper (1985) to enhance our access to the spiritual dimension in healing. Mercy as "the gentle rain from heaven" is an insightful metaphor that could serve as a focus or guiding image for the exercise.

- Take a deep breath, relax, and feel a sense of wholeness within yourself.
- Think of yourself or feel yourself as a system of energy rather than as a solid entity.
- Make the intent to attune to the spiritual consciousness, the source of universal love.
- Make the intent to be a conduit; that is, think of compassionate energy flowing into you from above and flowing out through you to the patient.

COMPASSION AND RESPECT

Compassion involves a respect for one's own wholeness and that of the patient. It also involves a respect for nursing. In Nightingale's view, nursing is working in cooperation with divine or natural laws to facilitate the evolution of human wholeness, the integration of body, mind, and spirit. For her, nothing in creation was more important than this. Unfortunately, modern society—including the health-care system—does not generally support her vision. Today most nurses work in institutions that value technology and cost-cutting far above nurturing, holistic care, and the prevention of disease.

Human society did not always devalue the process of nurturing wholeness. In early Greek civilization, for example, Hygeia was worshipped as a prominent goddess of healing. She was the virgin-mother, the compassionate nurturer, and facilitator of new life. As centuries passed, Hygeia's prominence was superceded by Asklepios, the god of medicine, and then eventually disappeared (Connell, 1983; Abrahamsen, 1997). At our time in history, however, there is a growing recognition of Hygeia's importance. For example, the ecology, holistic health, and world peace movements all share her view of the wholeness of the individual and the unity of all life. The nursing profession, in particular, can facilitate the return of Hygeia's image to prominence. As Connell (1983) has written:

> Each nurse can reclaim within him-or herself the image of Hygieia as she originally was, and each nurse can experience the inner attitude of independence, the gentle power and the specialized role as a nurturer and facilitator of new life. Each nurse can know, as he or she approaches a patient surrounded by the products of medical skill and technology, that within each patient viewed as a whole, life is continuously renewing itself, and that the focus of nursing is to tend this flow of new life. (p. 7)

REFERENCES

Abrahamsen, V. (1997). The goddess and healing: Nursing's heritage from antiquity. *Journal of Holistic Nursing, 15,* 9–24.

Arnold, E. (Trans.) (1885/1975). *The song celestial: A poetic version of the Bhagavad Gita.* Wheaton, IL: Theosophical Publishing.

Borysenko, J. (1998). Dialogues on science and mystery. In D. Ornish, *Love and survival.* New York: HarperPerennial.

Cohen, J. M., & Phipps, J-F. (1992) *The common experience.* Wheaton, IL: Quest Books.

Connell, M. T. (1983). Feminine consciousness and the nature of nursing practice. *Topics in Clinical Nursing, 5,* 1–10.

Cook, E. (1913). *The life of Florence Nightingale* (2 vols.). New York: Macmillan.

Dolan, J., et al. (1983). *Nursing in society: An historical perspective.* Philadelphia: W.B. Saunders.

Feng, G., & English, J. (Trans.) (1972). *Tao Te Ching.* New York: Vintage Books.

Huxley, A. (1945). *The perennial philosophy.* New York: Harper and Row.

Khema, A. (1991). *When the iron eagle flies: Buddhism for the West.* London: Arkana.

Kunz, D., & Peper, E. (1985). Fields and their clinical implications. In D. Kunz (Ed.), *Spiritual healing.* Wheaton, IL: Theosophical Publishing.

Owens, C. M. (1972). The mystical experience: Facts and values. In John White (Ed.), *The highest state of consciousness.* New York: Doubleday.

Quinn, J. (1981). Client care and nurse involvement in a holistic framework. In Dolores Krieger, *Foundations of holistic health nursing practices: The renaissance nurse.* Philadelphia: J.B. Lippincott.

6

Listening and Awareness

I n *Notes on Nursing* (1860/1969), Nightingale wrote that accurate observation lies at the foundation of scientifically based nursing practice. Through observation, aided by statistical analyses, we learn the natural laws of healing, or the "thoughts of God." It is the lack of accurate observation, she felt, which most impedes the development of nursing knowledge. In the following passage, she explains that we are so enmeshed in our own thoughts that we do not listen to the thoughts of God:

> What you "think" or what I "think" matters little. Let us see what God thinks. . . . God always justifies His ways. While we are thinking, He has been teaching. I have known cases of hospital pyaemia quite as severe in handsome private houses as in any of the worst hospitals, and from the same cause, viz., foul air. Yet nobody learnt the lesson. Nobody learnt *anything* at all from it. They went on *thinking*—thinking that the sufferer had scratched his thumb, or that it was singular that "all the servants" had "whitlows," or that something was "much about this year; there is always sickness in our house." This is a favourite mode of thought—leading not to inquire what is the uniform cause of these general "whitlows," but to stifle all inquiry. In what sense is "sickness" being "always there," a justification of its being "there" at all? (Nightingale, 1860/1969, p. 29)

The connection between a stagnant environment and the spread of infection is obvious to us now because it is a concept we learned in school. The principle underlying Nightingale's criticism, however, remains essential for nursing. Could we tell Nightingale today that we hear the voice of God more clearly than nurses a hundred years ago? That we are observing the healing process with perfect objectivity and insight? For Nightingale, the importance of accurate observation cannot be overestimated. In her chapter on the observation of the sick in *Notes on Nursing* (1860/1969), she came to the conclusion that "if you cannot get the habit of observation one way or other, you had better give up the being a nurse, for it is not your calling, however kind and anxious you may be" (p. 113).

From Nightingale's perspective, we unconsciously develop habitual and restrictive thinking patterns in response to society's expectations. In *Suggestions for Thought* (1860/1994), she made the following observation about conventional life in her day:

> Conventional life consists in this, in saying, "I am so sorry," "I hope you are coming," when we are not "sorry" and we do not "hope;" in *saying the proper thing without feeling it.* This is the first step in conventional life. The next step is when we actually do not know whether we feel it or not. And the last is when we have said what is "proper" till we do not know that we do not feel it—when we really think we feel a thing, because we have said it. (p. 139)

All the exercises described in this text can help us relax, focus, and be present in the moment so that our observing and listening skills will become more accurate. In addition, the regular practice of the mindfulness meditation exercise and the inner guide imagery exercise, both described in this chapter, can help us become more aware of the creative inner voice of our own higher consciousness.

MINDFULNESS

Within all the great spiritual traditions, the divine consciousness is described as the ultimate source of wisdom, understanding, and creative insight (Smith, 1991). This dimension of awareness transcends both space and time, thus it is not bound by the limitations of our personal experience. It is sometimes referred to as the "witness" consciousness, because it stands outside of our everyday life. Even more important, it is unconditioned by our habitual thinking patterns. Thus, it offers a clear, insightful, and creative assessment both of external circumstances and internal states of being.

Mindfulness or insight meditation, as developed in the Buddhist tradition, helps us attune to the higher, witness consciousness through the practice of nonjudgmental awareness (Goldstein, 1976). It is an exercise in objective observation. We observe, in a nonjudgmental manner, all the thoughts, emotions, and physical sensations that come into awareness. Unlike concentrative meditation (see Chapter 4) in which the mind has a single focus and all else is a distraction, mindfulness involves observing with equanimity everything that comes into awareness, moment by moment. Through this process of observation, we gradually become aware of our habitual thought processes and emotional reactions. And with this growing awareness, we are less inclined to overidentify with these personal processes and are able to perceive from a broader and clearer perspective. Mindfulness thus helps us practice nursing in the *holistic mode* (see chapter 5), which requires an awareness of the patient's state of being and our personal responses.

A long-range goal of mindfulness is the profound realization that one *is* the *witness consciousness*. It is one's own true nature. From Nightingale's perspective, it is the divine nature that exists within every human being. And when one is able to identify with this transcendent perspective, Nightingale wrote, one can "see as God sees, which is 'truth' " (*Suggestions for Thought*, 1860/1994, p. 143).

Mindfulness in Clinical Practice

The practice of mindfulness is an integral part of the 8-week stress reduction programs at the Stress Reduction Clinic of the University of Massachusetts Medical Center. Jon Kabat-Zinn, the director of the clinic, writes that mindfulness helps patients live more fully in the present moment:

In addition to having fewer symptoms, people experience improvements in health-related attitudes and behaviors and in how they view themselves, and the world. They report feeling more self-confident, assertive, and motivated to take better care of themselves and more confident of their ability to respond effectively in stressful circumstances. They also feel a greater sense of control in their lives, an increased willingness to look at stressful events as challenges rather than threats, and a greater sense of meaning in life. Our follow-up studies show that the majority keep up their mindfulness meditation practice in one way or another . . . for up to four years, and report continuing benefits from what they learned in the program. (Kabat-Zinn, 1992, p. 268)

A Mindfulness Exercise

The practice of mindfulness involves standing back, so to speak, and becoming aware of our bodies and minds *in the present moment*:

- Sit comfortably, relax, and close your eyes.
- Start by focusing your awareness on your breathing. Don't try to breathe in any particular way, just be aware of your breathing.
- When physical sensations arise, be aware of them.
- When you experience waves of emotion, don't judge them or become involved with them. Simply be aware of them.
- When thoughts arise, just acknowledge them as they pass through your mind.

Venerable Henepola Gunaratana (1991) in his discussion of mindfulness practice, advises us neither to cling to anything nor reject anything:

Let come what comes, and accommodate yourself to that, whatever it is. If good mental images arise, that is fine. If bad mental images arise, that is fine too. Look on all of it as equal, and make yourself comfortable with whatever happens. Don't fight with what you experience, just observe it all mindfully. (p. 46)

The practice of mindfulness help us to transcend the sympathetic mode and the defensive mode, the clinging and rejecting behavior that can lower the quality of patient care. Mindfulness brings us back to the stillness at the depth of our consciousness, which is beyond the clinging and rejecting at the personal level. And from this place of inner stillness, we can begin to work in the holistic mode, the mode of awareness and compassion.

Expanding Awareness

As mindfulness helps to expand one's awareness of reality, it is not uncommon for practitioners to have occasional "paranormal" or psychic experiences, such as the seeing of subtle energies, mental telepathy, precognitive episodes, and so on. Generally speaking, it cannot be predicted if and when these phenomena will occur. As there is an intrinsic order within the process of spiritual development, they often come when they can be most helpful to the individual. The advice of most instructors is to regard psychic phenomena as a mixed blessing, to appreciate the experiences and let them go.

On the one hand, there is much that we can learn from them. A telepathic experience, for example, can help us realize that our thought processes are not completely sealed within our brains but are connected with those of other people. Thus, it reinforces a concept that is found in all spiritual traditions: the underlying unity of all life. It is not uncommon for nurses to suddenly think of a patient in another room who is found to be in need of immediate help. In instances such as this, a telepathic experience can be life saving as well as educational.

On the other hand, giving undue attention to unusual psychic experiences can inflate the personal ego and distract us from out true purpose. Students who experience these phenomena can develop a false sense of superiority while those who do not can be unnecessarily discouraged. We must remember that psychic abilities and experiences are not the goal of spiritual development, nor do they form reliable criteria for evaluating our progress. Our goal is to connect our personal consciousness with the creative wisdom of a higher dimension. It is this wisdom that will help us evaluate and assimilate all experiences—normal and paranormal alike.

LISTENING TO GOD

Nightingale's perspective is consistent with the theory underlying mindfulness because she felt that the clarity of the divine consciousness is within us all. Indeed, in her view all great achievements in every field of endeavor are due to the divine spirit working through humanity. As can be seen in the following passage from *Suggestions for Thought* (1860/1994), she had little patience for personal egotism in this regard:

> How disgusting is the narrow selfish folly of A, who is contending in angry pages that he, and not B, made a certain discovery! Be assured it was neither A nor B—it was mankind, it was God in man. (p. 26)

Nightingale felt "it was mankind" because human progress is evolutionary. All great achievements are built upon humanity's previous efforts. She felt "it was God in man" because the fundamental inspiration comes from the Holy Spirit, the divine element within human nature.

From Nightingale's perspective, the voice of the Holy Spirit is a manifestation of divine law. If we discover and create the appropriate circumstances, the whole of our lives could be lived under its influence.

> It used to be thought that God spoke occasionally to individuals, with no other condition than that it was His arbitrary will so occasionally to speak—that He called man out of his sleep with no reference to any particular state in man, the consequences of which would be always communication of the divine in man with God. . . . We believe, from experience, that man is capable of living always, as it were, in a state of reference to that Higher Being. (*Suggestions for Thought*, pp. 128–9)

What is the "particular state" that enables us to hear the inner divine voice? This is the question that Nightingale asks us to address. The most obvious response is that it is *a state of inner quietude*. We have to be quiet and listen with an open mind. The individual who reported the spiritual experience presented in chapter 3 was in an excellent state of mind for a fresh insight. He or she was "confused and questing" and prayed with "unashamed sincerity" for a greater degree of understanding. The answer was the spontaneous experience of heightened spiritual awareness.

Don Juan's Exercise

The necessity and the difficulty of listening are described by Carlos Castaneda (1971), who was an apprentice of the shaman, Don Juan. Healing and other works performed by shamans require an altered state of consciousness which Carlos was not achieving to his satisfaction. When he asked Don Juan the reason for his lack of progress, the old man told Carlos that he must learn to stop the incessant *internal talk* that was reinforcing his limited personal view of reality:

> Whenever we finish talking to ourselves, the world is always as it should be. We renew it, we kindle it with life, we uphold it with our internal talk. Not only that, but we also choose our paths as we talk to ourselves. Thus we repeat the same choices over and over until the day we die, because we keep on repeating the same internal talk over and over until the day we die.
> A warrior is aware of this and strives to stop his talking. (p. 218)

Carlos was given an exercise to help stop his internal talking. He had to sit quietly with his eyes closed and "listen to the sounds of the world." This exercise is similar to concentrative meditation because he had to keep his mind focused on external sounds. It is also similar to mindfulness because he had to acknowledge each sound as it presented itself, moment by moment.

At first the exercise was excruciating for Carlos, but eventually he attained a state of inner quietude so his inner development could proceed. Even though most of us will never apprentice ourselves to a shaman, we all share the problem of upholding the world with our internal talk. Thus we can all benefit from Don Juan's exercise. If, even for a moment, we can suspend or get beyond our habitual flow of opinions, we can be open to a new way of seeing.

The Inner Guide Exercise

The *inner guide* is a widely used exercise that helps to strengthen the communication between the personal self and the spiritual consciousness. It can be used before making decisions, or as a daily meditation to enhance your level of integration:

• Sit quietly with your eyes closed, take a deep breath, and relax.
• Make the intent to connect with the source of highest wisdom within yourself.
• Visualize yourself climbing up a high hill where you can see clearly in all directions. (This is, of course, a metaphor for the broader perspective of our higher consciousness; from that level we can see open roads, dead ends, and potentially dangerous situations which are out of the line of vision of our ordinary waking consciousness.)
• Try to put aside your preconceived opinions and listen quietly in the stillness. If a symbol of your higher consciousness (such as a wise old man or woman) spontaneously appears, you could ask a question and listen for the response, and even engage in a dialogue.

The *inner guide* can be seen as a form of mindfulness because one *listens* in a nonjudgmental manner. It can also be viewed as both an active and passive imagery exercise. *Active imagery* is imagery that is consciously constructed for a therapeutic purpose. For example, in previous chapters we have used the image of white light to help us connect with the spiritual energy, and the image of a peaceful place to help evoke a state of physical relaxation. *Receptive imagery* consists of images that are not deliberately constructed; they *bubble up,* or *flow into,* the conscious mind (Achterberg, Dossey, & Kolkmeier, 1994). The *inner guide* incorporates both types of imagery because one consciously visualizes oneself in a place that is receptive to images from the spirit.

The *inner guide* exercise is a useful strategy for patients, as an aid in making decisions and in learning from their illnesses. Many patients are faced with serious decisions regarding their courses of treatment. The wisdom of the higher consciousness can provide guidance in answering questions such as this. The exercise can also be used to facilitate personal growth during a time of illness. The spiritual level is our most profound source of wisdom. Enhancing our connection with this dimension, therefore, opens our eyes to the meaning of all life's events, including illnesses, and the lessons we can learn from them. Illness can provide a good opportunity for growth because it tends to disrupt many habitual patterns; therefore, new healthier patterns can be established if appropriate help is available.

The Simontons' Use of the Inner Guide

The Simonton program for patients with cancer is a good illustration of a holistic approach to care that includes the *inner guide* exercise (Simonton et al., 1978). This program represents one of the first successful attempts to integrate traditional medical and complementary modalities. The program received a great deal of publicity and sparked a widespread interest among health professionals in the use of imagery (Rossman, 1993). The Simontons' approach, inspired by research in biofeedback, is based on the concept that the mind has an impact on the body. Psychological patterns contribute both to the development and the alleviation of disease processes.

Imagery, a central component of the Simonton program, is used in four ways:

• Patients are taught to use imagery to evoke a general relaxation response.
• Patients learn ways of evoking specific physiological responses. For example, they learn to *see* the medical treatments and their immune systems as organized and powerful, overcoming the cancer which they *see* as weak and confused.
• Patients draw pictures of themselves and their illnesses as an aid in evaluating the effectiveness of the program. If, for example, a patient draws the cancer cells as bigger than the white cells, it might indicate that this individual needs help with issues of self-confidence, inner strength, or empowerment.
• Patients learn the *inner guide* exercise to access, in a conscious manner, the wisdom of the *higher consciousness*.

Gwen, one of the Simontons' patients, reported that a figure named Dr. Fritz spontaneously appeared during an *inner guide* exercise. The Simontons describe her interactions with this figure (Simonton et al., 1978):

> When she had asked Dr. Fritz what he was doing in her imagery, he reported that he was there to help her regain her health. She then asked him a series of questions, and his answers indicated a deep understanding of the emotional issues Gwen had avoided facing in working with us.
>
> She would listen to Dr. Fritz. She might, for example, have a telephone conversation with her daughter about an upcoming visit, a conversation which left her quite angry. She wouldn't say anything about the anger to her daughter, but later in the day she would begin having pain from her cancer. She consulted with Dr. Fritz about her pain, and he informed her that it resulted from not having dealt directly with her daughter. She was feeling resentful of her daughter's demands on her time, Dr. Fritz stated, and if she wanted to get rid of her pain she needed to phone her daughter and tell her she was not coming for the weekend. When Gwen called her daughter and canceled the visit, her pain began to go away. She reported a number of such incidents—perhaps thirty or forty over a period of six months—and her health improved steadily. (pp. 202–203)

From a spiritual perspective, Dr. Fritz was a personification of the *higher consciousness*. We do not know why it manifested in this way. Perhaps it chose a form and manner that would be most acceptable to the patient. In any case, this is a very good example of an effective insight: the patient was willing to listen; the message was truthful, clear, and presented in a helpful manner; the patient trusted the insight enough to act upon it; and the result was an improvement in both physical and psychological health.

Through the regular use of strategies such as the *inner guide* exercise, the personality begins to absorb the values of the *higher consciousness*. The two begin to merge. To use the above case as an example, Gwen would begin by saying "I feel pain and Dr. Fritz tells me the cause of it and how to get rid of it." Gradually she would identify with or integrate the point of view of Dr. Fritz. She would end by saying "*I know* that when I let people impose on me I feel angry and my body reacts in pain." It is this linking or binding of the personality and the *higher consciousness* that constitutes the process of spiritual development.

Answers from the Spirit

After hearing an explanation of the *inner guide* exercise, a student exclaimed: "I'm afraid of what it might tell me!" This would be a legitimate fear if *it* were an external, capricious force. As mentioned before, the inner divine consciousness is *oneself*, one's own deepest nature. When we open our minds in quietude, its insights come with a sense of peace and rightness. Nightingale emphasized this in *Suggestions for Thought* (1860/1994), writing that we should not think of submitting to the will of God, but of being in accordance with it:

> "Submitting to God's will" is a phrase we cannot understand. It is as if you looked upon God as something apart, *without,* independent of all principle, to whom you have only to submit. But if, for "God," we read "the spirit of perfect love and wisdom," how can we talk about *submitting* to perfect love, directed by wisdom: We accord with it; we don't submit. (p. 125)

It is important to keep in mind that the *higher consciousness* tends to communicate in symbols. Unlike a sign, which has a literal meaning, a symbol represents an immaterial or multidimensional quality. For example, if you dream about a particular person, ask yourself: what qualities does this person embody? What are my associations with this person? What part of myself might this person symbolize?

There are many ways that the *higher consciousness* responds to our questions. The following are some of the more common ones:

• *A strong hunch or gut feeling.* You may feel a deeper certainty about going in one direction as opposed to another, or a *gut feeling* that events will peacefully resolve themselves.

• *An inner voice.* In your mind's ear you may hear an inner voice, giving a message that is clear and complete, simple and helpful. Nightingale heard an inner voice on four occasions, calling her to God's service (Cook, 1913). You can rest assured, however, that not every message is as dramatic as this!

• *A symbolic image.* In your mind's eye you may see an image that has meaningful associations for you. A colleague of mine reported seeing an image of a Ford Model-T spontaneously appear to his inner vision. He interpreted this to mean that his approach to a particular issue was outmoded, and that he should investigate some newly developed strategies.

• *A dream.* Dreams arise from different dimensions of consciousness. Some chaotic dreams are due to a physiological disturbance, such as indigestion; others are associated with a release of anxiety. Some dreams arise from the spiritual dimension. From the Jungian perspective (Jung, 1964), dreams from the higher level frequently contain a symbol of wisdom and power such as a person of stature, a crystal or significant animal, or a witness or commenting voice. These dreams generally have an ordered configuration or sequence, and can even be precognitive because they arise from a level of consciousness that transcends time.

The following is a good example of a dream that originated from a higher level of consciousness. The dreamer was a man in his mid-forties who had just received a diagnosis of metastatic melanoma. Marie-Louise von Franz, a well-known Jungian analyst, describes his dream:

> He saw a green, half-high, not-yet-ripe wheat field. A herd of cattle had broken into the field and trampled down and destroyed everything in it. Then a voice from above called out: "Everything seems to be destroyed, but from the roots under the earth the wheat will grow again (von Franz, 1986, p. 10).

Here we see the *higher consciousness* calling out to the man, telling him that his untimely death will not destroy his existence, but that his invisible source or essence will manifest again. Dr. von Franz wrote that the man did not accept this interpretation of the dream, and unfortunately he died shortly thereafter in a state of inner conflict.

• *A synchronistic experience.* Synchronicity is a descriptive term for the link between two events that are connected through their *meaning,* a link that cannot be explained by cause and effect. It requires a human participant to acknowledge the connection between these events (Bolan, 1979). A synchronistic experience is, thus, a meaningful coincidence. For example, a few years ago I was having difficulty completing a writing project and repeated the *inner guide* exercise several times. Within a 24-hour period two individuals, independently and without any knowledge of the writing problem, mentioned *A Room of One's Own* by Virginia Woolf. I bought the book, trusting that this strange coincidence was the answer, and found within the solution to my "writers' block."

God's Voice or Ours?

Nightingale asks us to investigate whether or not our inner voice is authentic, that is, "whether it is I who speak, or whether it is God speaking to me" (*Suggestions for Thought,* p. 127). This is a difficult issue, because our personal "internal talk" can so easily block and distort the voice of the spirit. As Nightingale comments:

> We may naturally be mistaken in what God says to us, because we have to construct for ourselves and each other the vessel into which the Holy Ghost enters, and often inevitably it becomes occupied with other ghosts. (*Suggestions for Thought,* 1860/1994, p. 25)

This is the same principle that we discussed in chapter 2 with respect to the scriptures. From Nightingale's perspective, the writers of holy texts had their own "internal talk" and were also conditioned by the culture of their time. It was for this reason she felt all sacred texts should be critically evaluated.

What are some of the criteria by which we can evaluate our own inner voice? How can we tell, for example, if a hunch is a real insight and not an emotional impulse? This is the question most frequently asked about the *inner guide* exercise. In general, an insight "rings true" from within; it is clear and complete, and it is also lasting. An emotional impulse tends to fade or change over time and, if we had acted upon it, we often have regrets. A wise old friend of mine used to give the following advice: "If you feel drawn to make a certain decision, test yourself by 'trying it on,' so to speak. Pretend your decision is final and see how it feels after a few days. If you are still comfortable with it, you know you are on the right track, but if you have a sense of growing unease you know that something is wrong and that more evaluation and meditation are necessary."

A true insight will not be in conflict with your highest ethical standards. Indeed, from the spiritual perspective we have an awareness of the interrelationship of all things, so that our welfare and that of the world is the same. All the great spiritual traditions teach that compassion, understanding, and generosity are characteristic of the transformed human being. If we follow our inner guidance we may disappoint certain people, however. Nightingale's mother, for example, was extremely upset when her daughter chose a life of nursing instead of high society. But from Nightingale's point of view, we do not come into the world to please other people; we come here to fulfill our inner purpose.

It is sometimes mistakenly thought that, if we sincerely try to listen and follow our inner guidance, all difficulties will miraculously dematerialize. It is true that our path through life will become much smoother and happier, because the inner wisdom will prevent us from shortsighted actions with their unpleasant consequences. There are many forces in both nature and society, however, that we cannot personally control. Difficulties will arise. But we can meet them calmly, with the vision, confidence, and resilience that the inner divine consciousness gives us.

A Clinical Example

The inner voice of insight is integral to nursing practice. Benner (1984) observes that making intuitive decisions by drawing on knowledge and experience is characteristic of expert nursing. Nursing research provides us with knowledge. It is wisdom that helps us utilize the knowledge appropriately. The following is an example from Benner's (1984) qualitative study:

> I took care of a patient, a very likable young physician, who had an open-and-close exploratory laparotomy for pancreatic cancer. He had been febrile. For three nights I woke him every four hours and helped him do all his breathing exercises and lung physical therapy. He was

really depressed and wasn't talking about anything that had to do with his diagnosis and everything that was happening to him. The fourth night that I was on, his temperature came down some, and by now he was exhausted from lack of sleep. I figured that he was going to have a lot better chance to focus on things that he needed and wanted to focus on if he could just get some uninterrupted sleep. His temperature remained the same in the morning. His lungs probably would have been clearer had I awakened him at 3 AM, but I elected not to, given his extreme fatigue and depression. It's not clear what is the right thing to do. There are little studies done about the effectiveness of chest physical therapy and then there are other studies done about the effectiveness of sleep. But there is never anything that proves that X is better than Y, especially in a particular situation. . . . It is expected that I will use my best judgment under the circumstances (pp. 140–1).

This nurse's best judgment under the circumstances was based on: (a) an awareness of the inconclusive research findings, (b) a mindfulness of the patient's total state of being, (c) knowledge based on previous experience, and (d) an intuitive feeling about the best course of action at that moment.

REFERENCES

Achterberg, J., Dossey, B., & Kolkmeier, L. (1994). *Rituals of healing: Using imagery for health and wellness.* New York: Bantam Books.

Bennner, P. (1984). *From novice to expert: Excellence and power in clinical nursing practice.* Menlo Park, CA: Addison-Wesley.

Bolan, J. (1979). *The tao of psychology: Synchronicity and the self.* San Francisco: Harper & Row.

Calabria, M., & Macrae, J. (1994) *Suggestions for Thought by Florence Nightingale: Selections and commentaries.* Philadelphia: University of Pennsylvania Press.

Carson, V. (1989). Spirituality and the nursing process. In V. Carson (Ed.), *Spiritual dimensions of nursing practice.* Philadelphia: W.B. Saunders.

Castaneda, C. (1971). *A separate reality: Further conversations with Don Juan.* New York: Simon and Schuster.

Cook, E. (1913). *The life of Florence Nightingale* (2 vols.). New York: Macmillan.

Dossey, B., Keegan, L., & Guzzetta, C. (2000). *Holistic nursing: A handbook for practice* (3rd ed.). Gaithersburg, MD: Aspen Publications.

Goldstein, J. (1976). *The experience of insight: a natural unfolding.* Santa Cruz, CA: Unity Press.

Gunaratana, H. (1991). *Mindfulness in plain English.* Boston: Wisdom Publications.

Jung, C., von Franz, M. L., Henderson, J., Jacobi, J., & Jaffe, A. (1964). *Man and his symbols.* Garden City, NY: Doubleday.

Kabat-Zinn, J. (1993). Mindfulness meditation: Health benefits of an ancient Buddhist practice. In D. Goleman & J. Gurin (Eds.). *Mind-body medicine* (pp. 259–275). Yonkers, NY: Consumer Reports Books.

O'Brien, M.E. (1999). *Spirituality in nursing: Standing on holy ground.* Sudbury, MA: Jones and Bartlett.

Rossman, L. (1993). *Imagery: Learning to use the mind's eye.* In D. Goleman & J. Gurin (Eds.), *Mind-body medicine* (pp. 291–300). Yonkers, NY: Consumer Reports Books.

Simonton, O.C., Simonton, S., & Creighton, J. (1978). *Getting well again.* New York: Bantam Books.

Smith, H. (1991). *The world's religions.* New York: HarperCollins

von Franz, M.L. (1986). *On dreams and death.* Boston: Shambhala Publications.

7

On Prayer

❦

Nightingale was particularly drawn to Socrates' short prayer at the end of Plato's *Phaedrus*: "Beloved Pan, and all ye other gods who haunt this place, give me beauty in the inward soul; and may the outward and inward man be at one." She told her friend Benjamin Jowett that this prayer contained at least half of the spiritual teachings of the great mystic St. John of the Cross (Cook, 1913).

Prayer, from Nightingale's perspective, is the process of linking the outward personal self with the inward divine spirit. It is the alignment of our thoughts, feelings, and actions with the consciousness of God, or divine spirit within. "What [God] desires seems to be accordance with Him, that we should be one with Him, not prostrate before Him (*Suggestions for Thought*, 1860/1994, p. 125).

A contemplative prayer exercise, designed to help us experience the inner presence of God, is described in a subsequent section. However, Nightingale felt that the forms and possibilities of prayer, as a process of inner integration, are limitless. With respect to nursing, for example, profound reflection on the laws of healing, striving to "see as God sees," is a form of prayer. Feeling compassion for all those in need, thereby aligning our emotions with the Divine Spirit that embraces all things, is also a form of prayer. Working in harmony with the laws of God can transform our physical actions into prayer. Indeed, Nightingale wrote "that it is a religious act to clean out a gutter and to prevent cholera, and that it is not a religious act to pray (in the sense of asking)" (Quinn & Prest, 1987, p. 18).

Petitionary Prayer

Nightingale criticized the concept of petitionary prayer because she thought it was inconsistent with universal law. Effects arise only when the appropriate causes have been established.

For example, in Nightingale's era, outbreaks of cholera and dysentery were a major health problem. Clergymen preached "cholera sermons," and people fasted and prayed for divine intervention (Dossey, 1999). Nightingale, studying her statistical tables, saw a connection between these diseases and a lack of proper sewage management. Her conclusions were that this connection illustrates a divine or natural law, and the way to promote health is not to sit and pray, but to work in harmony with God's laws, which, in this case, means improving sanitary conditions.

In *Suggestions for Thought (1860/1994)* she wrote:

> It did strike me as odd, sometimes, that we should pray to be delivered from 'plague, pestilence, and famine,' when all the common sewers ran into the Thames, and fevers haunted undrained land, and the districts which cholera would visit could be pointed out. I thought that cholera came that we might remove these causes, not pray that God would remove the cholera. (p. 126)

This idea is also conveyed in *Notes on Nursing* (1860/1969):

> God lays down certain physical laws. Upon his carrying out such laws depends our responsibility (that much abused word) . . . Yet we seem to be continually expecting that He will work a miracle—i.e., break his own laws expressly to relieve us of responsibility. (p. 25)

Today the leading cause of death in the United States is not infectious diseases, such as cholera, but heart disease. Following Nightingale's ideas, the underlying approach to controlling this disease is still the same. Scientific studies have demonstrated that heart disease is statistically correlated with a diet high in fat and low in fiber, a high level of stress, and a sedentary lifestyle. These correlations could be termed a physical law. The probability of developing heart disease will be lowered if we abide by the law, that is, if we eat a "heart healthy" diet, regulate our stress level, and engage in regular exercise. Research by Ornish (1990) has demonstrated that heart disease can actually be *reversed* through participation in a program that includes a low-fat, high-fiber diet; smoking cessation; an exercise regime; and stress regulation methods such as visualization, breathing techniques, meditation, and the acquisition of skills to identify and communicate feelings.

Prayers of Confession

In a universe regulated by universal law, there is no arbitrary punishment by God. Indeed, Nightingale wrote that the *universal divine mind,* that comprehends all, cannot possibly be personally offended by human actions. Painful consequences of sinful actions are the effects of law, not God's displeasure. Thus, asking for God's forgiveness, in Nightingale's view, is an inappropriate use of prayer: first, because God is not offended, and second, because in a lawful universe the effects of one's actions cannot be arbitrarily obliterated (*Suggestions for Thought,* 1860/1994, pp. 54–57).

Nightingale viewed sin as behavior that is not in harmony with the divine inner nature. From her point of view, sin is inevitable, given that human beings possess free will and are not completely unified with, and thus guided by, their inner God-consciousness. Sin, for Nightingale, is analogous to a mistake. It plays a role in the developmental process because it generates negative feedback. Painful consequences force us to reevaluate our behavior and modify our actions. It is this behavior modification, rather than prayer for forgiveness, which is the necessary response.

The teaching of God's eternal punishment for sin, which Nightingale called a "diabolical doctrine," is inconsistent with the major concepts in her philosophy, such as that of a compassionate *higher intelligence,* the unity of life, and spiritual development. In her view, the life process of the entire human race is moving toward higher levels of integration. Indeed, she wrote in *Suggestions for Thought* (1860/1994): "In accordance with God's law, human consciousness is tending to become what God's consciousness is—to become one with the consciousness of God" (p. 58).

Nightingale criticized the criminal justice system of her day because she felt it was associated with the concept of a punitive God and, moreover, that it delivered arbitrary and ineffective forms of punishment. From her perspective, the goal of punishment should be rehabilitation, in keeping with the ideal of spiritual development.

> The Court feels bound to pass a severe sentence,' what does that mean? And the criminal 'is imprisoned for eighteen calendar months,' what is that for?—merely to keep him out of mischief for that time? or to deter others by terror? Or to reform him? We know that the second of these objects is not attained, and the third is not even aimed at. Would it not be better to let him out? But no, 'the Court feels bound to pass a severe sentence' and God feels bound to give the sentence 'of everlasting chains under darkness.' Can He too only punish, instead of reforming: The idea of eternal damnation had its origin amid a society which exercised punishment; and as soon as mankind sees that there is no such word, that reformation is the only word, eternal punishment will disappear out of our religion; everlasting damnation and capital punishment will go out together. (*Suggestions for Thought*, 1860/1994), p. 91)

Nightingale felt that the real "punishment" for sin is not a fine or a jail term, but the inner fragmentation that is associated with it. The appropriate response, that will eventually lead to happiness, is to try to realign ourselves with the inner presence of God. In the following passage from *Suggestions for Thought* (1860/1994), she asks us to let go of our pangs of regret and look with confidence to the future:

> Away with regrets which have no true foundation, empty your heart of them! Work out the page of today with goodwill, even though the mistake of yesterday may have complicated it. . . . There is a higher, better, truer help than those pangs—you will never rise high goaded by them. Strive to awaken the divine spirit of love in yourself; to awaken it doing your present work, however you may have erred in the past—this will help you far better than dwelling on your own mistakes. There is nothing elevating or animating in the dissection of them. Essentially, in their very nature, they bring suffering or privation. Bear it in a true spirit and work on. Turn your mistake to as much account as you can, for the gaining of experience, but, above

all, yield not to paralyzing, depressing retrospection. God gives us the noble privilege of working out His work. He does not work for us. He gives us the means to find the way we should go. An eternal course is before us. (p. 96)

Contemplative Prayer

Contemplative prayer, as it is being revived in the Christian tradition, is consistent with Nightingale's developmental view of spirituality. In the words of Thomas Keating, a Cistercian priest and abbot, contemplative prayer is "the opening of mind and heart—our whole being—to God, the Ultimate Mystery, beyond thoughts, words, and emotions" (Keating, 1992, p. 138).

Lectio Divina

Contemplative prayer was an integral component of *lectio divina,* or divine reading, which was a common practice in the Christian church until the end of the Middle Ages. The practice of *lectio divina* was designed to help an individual move spontaneously through three stages, the third of which was contemplative:

• Reading and reflecting on the word of God in scripture;
• Making aspirations inspired by these reflections;
• Opening to inner silence and resting in the presence of God.

In the third phase of *lectio divina,* the intellect reaches its limit and then becomes still, listening, as it were, for the voice of God within. Keating (1992) writes that the third or contemplative phase became neglected after the Middle Ages because of the overly intellectual bias of Western culture, which represses the intuitive faculty, and also because of the anticontemplative trend of Christian teachings in recent centuries. He attributes the current renewal of interest in contemplative prayer to two factors:

1. Historical and theological studies have rediscovered the teachings of St. John of the Cross and other Christian masters of the spiritual life; and

2. Eastern methods of meditation similar to the Christian practice of contemplative prayer have proliferated, produced good results, and received much publicity.

CENTERING PRAYER

Keating (1992), one of the founders of the Centering Prayer Movement, explains that, in his experience, the practice of *lectio divina* can be difficult for modern Westerners because their overly active analytical processes impede the spontaneous movement from reading to contemplation. Centering prayer has been developed as a way of quieting the overactive intellect so that one can let go and move more easily into the peace and stillness of contemplative prayer. The guidelines for Centering Prayer are as follows:

- Choose a sacred word as the symbol of your intention to consent to God's presence and action within. Some examples are: peace, shalom, silence, Lord Jesus.
- Sit comfortably and with eyes closed, silently introduce the sacred word and keep it the focus of your attention.
- When you become aware of thoughts, return ever so gently to the sacred word.
- At the end of the prayer period, remain in silence with eyes closed for a couple of minutes.

Keating emphasizes the importance of one's *intent* when practicing Centering Prayer:

Centering prayer is not as much an exercise of attention as intention. It may take a while to grasp this distinction. You do not attend to any particular thought content. Rather, you *intend* to go to your inmost being, where you believe God dwells. You are opening to Him by pure faith, not by means of concepts or feelings. It is like knocking gently on a door. You are not pounding on the door with your faculties as if to say, "Open in the name of the law! I demand that you let me in!" You can't force this door. It opens from the other side. What you are saying by means of the sacred word is, "Here I am, waiting." It's a waiting game to the nth degree. Nothing flashy is going to happen, or, if it does, you should gently return to the sacred word. Even if you have a vision or hear infused words, you should return to the sacred word. This is the essence of the method. (pp. 39–40)

Keating (1992) recommends practicing for a minimum of 20 minutes twice a day. For centering prayer, like Eastern methods of meditation, is a discipline. In *Suggestions for Thought* (1860/1994) Nightingale used athletic training as a metaphor. "There are definite means," she wrote, "of acquiring spiritual nerve and sinew as well as bodily" (p. 119). We do not expect to grow in any athletic skill without regular exercise; neither can we expect to grow in grace without the appropriate effort. Even though the divine presence is beyond our thoughts and conscious control, Nightingale would remind us of two things: we live in a lawful universe and we have the force of spiritual evolution behind us. *You can't force this door.* But if you put yourself in the right condition, you will greatly increase the probability that it will open.

REFERENCES

Calabria, M., & Macrae, J. (Eds.). (1994). *Suggestions for thought by Florence Nightingale: Selections and commentaries.* Philadelphia: University of Pennsylvania Press.

Cook, E. (1913). *The life of Florence Nightingale* (2 vols.). New York: Macmillan.

Dossey, B. (1999). *Florence Nightingale: Mystic, visionary, and healer.* Springhouse, PA: Springhouse.

Jowett, B. (1860). On the interpretation of scripture. In *Essays and Reviews.* London: John W. Parker and Son.

Keating, T. (1992). *Open mind, open heart: The contemplative dimension of the gospel.* New York: Continuum Publishing.

Nightingale, F. (1969). *Notes on nursing.* New York: Dover Publications.

Ornish, D. (1990). *Dr. Dean Ornish's program for reversing heart disease.* New York: Ballantine Books.

Quinn, E., & Prest, J. (Eds.) (1987). *Dear Miss Nightingale: A selection of Benjamin Jowett's letters: 1860–1893.* Oxford: Clarendon Press.

Rahula, W. (1959). *What the Buddha taught.* New York: Grove Press.

Woodham-Smith, C. (1957). *Florence Nightingale: 1820–1910.* New York: McGraw-Hill.

8

Spirituality and Conduct

All the great religions of the world provide teachings, or precepts, to guide behavior. Within the Judeo-Christian tradition, for example, we have the Ten Commandments that Moses brought down from the mountain, and Jesus' injunction that we do unto others as we would have them do unto us. Muslims recognize the teachings of both Moses and Jesus, and they believe that the behavioral guidelines in the Koran covering such matters as almsgiving, prayer, and fasting, are a continuation of the revelations in the Old and New Testaments (Gerardi, 1989; Smith, 1991).

The ethical guidelines of *Ashtanga (Eight-limbed) Yoga* are similar to those of the Western traditions. *Yama* means abstinence or restraint: it requires that one abstain from violence, lying, stealing, sexual misconduct, and possessiveness or acquisitiveness. *Niyama* refers to observances: the cultivation of love, contentment, purity, self-discipline, and the study of universal truths.

The most obvious rationale for good conduct is its effect on human society. Society would quickly disintegrate if the majority of people routinely engaged in lying, stealing, and violence. Although great acts of heroism occur during times of disintegration, such as war, it is a peaceful society that best facilitates the unfolding of the higher qualities of the spirit.

An equally important rationale is the effect of conduct on an individual's inner development. Good or moral conduct can facilitate the integration process by supporting a dynamic resonance between the personal self and the spirit. For example, if the divine consciousness is the essence of truth, then speaking truthfully puts us in harmony with the spirit. It strengthens the bond between the individual and the universal. Lying, on the other hand, is a behavior that is not consistent with the divine consciousness; thus, it tends to disrupt the inner process of binding oneself to the spirit. Again, if the spiritual consciousness is the essence of love and unity, then compassionate action tends to strengthen the bond while violent or harmful forms of behavior tend to disrupt it. As we discussed in Chapter 7, the real "punishment" for negative behavior is not a fine or jail term, but the inner fragmentation that comes as a natural consequence.

ON REWARD AND PUNISHMENT

A teaching common to some religions is that the good will go to heaven and the bad will go to hell. But what is heaven? And what is hell? Are they actual places, or states of being, or both?

In the Gnostic Gospel of St. Thomas (Pagels, 1981) Jesus intimated that the Kingdom of Heaven is symbolic of a transformed state of consciousness:

> The Kingdom of the Father is spread out upon the earth, and men do not see it. . . .
> When you make the two one, and when you make the inside like the outside and the outside like the inside, and the above like the below, and when you make the male and the female one and the same . . . then you will enter [the Kingdom]. (p. 155)

Interestingly, this statement is highly consistent with Nightingale's definition of religion as the process of binding the personal self (the *below*) with the spiritual consciousness (the *above*). It is also consistent with Jung's theory of individuation. The first phase of the individuation process is the acceptance and integration of the *shadow*, or those *personal characteristics that we do not like and would prefer to ignore* (see chapter 4). The next step of the individuation process is for a man to integrate his feminine side and a women her masculine side; that is, men enhance qualities such as intuition, sensitivity to feelings, and a connectedness to the earth, while women enhance qualities such as assertiveness, physical power, logical reasoning, and the ability to establish and achieve personal goals. From the Jungian perspective, we become whole or individuated when we *bind* the shadow, the masculine and the feminine, and the personal ego with the transcendent self (von Franz, 1964). Thus it is through the realization of wholeness that we can see the Kingdom of Heaven *here and now,* "spread out upon the earth."

The traditional teaching of heaven and hell as locations of eternal reward or punishment was challenged by Frederick Denison Maurice, a Broad Church Anglican and friend of Nightingale's. In his *Theological Essays,* he wrote that punishment for evil conduct is not a specific place called *hell* but an inner state of alienation from God: "Eternal punishment is the punishment of being without the knowledge of God, who is love, and of Jesus who manifested it; even as eternal life is declared to be the having of the knowledge of God and Jesus Christ" (p. 307).

Because Maurice's opinion was considered immoral by the Church of England, he was forced to resign from his position as Professor of Theology at King's College. Nightingale was so upset when she heard about this that she considered leaving the Church of England (Goldie, 1983, 3.F4, 763), for her own opinion was entirely consistent with that of Maurice. In the following passage from *Suggestions for Thought* (1860/1994), she explains that goodness brings us closer to God, the source of happiness. Eternal happiness is, thus, not a reward meted out by a capricious god that can change its mind at our personal request (a teaching that she considered "immoral"), but a state of being that we consciously achieve through the application of natural laws.

> Can a doctrine be immoral where goodness *is* happiness, not connected with it or the cause of it, but identical with it?—where wickedness is misery? The other doctrine says that there is always a hope that God will forgive—that we may sin and escape the punishment. But the only happiness worth having is God's happiness; and the divine happiness, that happiness which we are *all* to share, is not the consequence of goodness; it is goodness. But where happiness is made to depend upon some change of mind in God, and not in

man—where, as in the case of the dying but repentant sinner, God is supposed to forgive, that is, to change His mind towards him, and bestow happiness as an arbitrary gift—can there exist than this any more immoral doctrine? God gives us nothing. We are to work out a happiness, like His, in ourselves, in accordance with His laws. (p. 76)

The story of the penitent thief who was crucified next to Jesus is often used as an example of the mercy and forgiveness of God. Nightingale's interpretation of this story, quoted below, provides a fine illustration of her understanding of universal law, spiritual development, and life after death. The thief's spiritual perception should bring him great happiness in the afterlife. His thievery, however, demonstrates a degree of alienation from God that will detract from his happiness. In the afterlife, just as on earth, we must work to turn all evil into good.

It is very evident that the man was far from being all evil. The very high state of spiritual perception necessary to believe in Christ's kingdom at a moment when his nearest friends considered their hopes blasted and his kingdom destroyed; to pray not for life, not for being saved from the cross, but only for moral salvation, shows that he was already very far on the road to happiness. As far then as he was right he will enjoy happiness, identical with the right. *In his wrong,* not *for* his wrong, he will suffer till his evil becomes all good. (*Suggestions for Thought,* 1860/1994, p. 52)

POTENTIAL PITFALLS OF THE PRECEPTS

Observing religious precepts or moral guidelines should bring us closer to the inner divine spirit. Like all spiritual practices, they are a means to a greater end. Problems arise, however, when the end is forgotten and the means become the main focus. For example, making religious behavior an end in itself can create divisiveness and a false sense of superiority. One looks down on those who do not seem to be observing the guidelines as well as oneself. This attitude is, of course, contrary to the spiritual consciousness which is unitive and compassionate.

Sometimes precepts and religious observances can become a means not to a greater, but to a lesser, end. For example, one can behave in a religious manner to win approval from others or to gain prestige. In this case one's behavior aggrandizes the personal self and thus hinders, rather than facilitates, spiritual development.

Jesus warned his followers about these pitfalls in the following passage from the Gospel of Matthew:

> Be sure you do not perform your acts of piety before men, for them to watch . . . when thou givest alms, do not sound a trumpet before thee, as the hypocrites do in synagogues and in streets, to win the esteem of men. Believe me, they have their reward already. But when thou givest alms, thou shalt not so much as let thy left hand know that thy right hand is doing, so secret is thy almsgiving to be; and then thy Father, who sees what is done in secret, will reward thee.
>
> Do not lay up treasure for yourselves on earth, where there is moth and rust to consume it, where there are thieves to break in and steal it; lay up treasure for yourselves in heaven, where there is not moth or rust to consume it, no thieves to break in and steal. Where your treasure-house is, there your heart is too. (verse 6)

Because of the dangers of overfocusing on behavior, some traditions, such as Zen Buddhism, do not emphasize moral or ethical practices. In one of his talks on the practice of Zazen (sitting with a still mind) Roshi Suzuki (1970) explains that it is our separation from the unitive, creative consciousness or "original mind" that creates the need for precepts. When we connect with our inner spiritual nature, we have a sense of self-sufficiency. Thus the personal desires that often motivate unethical actions lose their power, and our actions become spontaneously good.

> For Zen students the most important thing is not to be dualistic. Our "original mind" includes everything within itself. It is always rich and sufficient within itself. You should not lose your self-sufficient state of mind. This does not mean a closed mind, but actually an empty mind and a ready mind. If your mind is empty, it is always ready for anything; it is open to everything. . . .
>
> If you discriminate too much, you limit yourself. If you are too demanding or too greedy, your mind is not rich and self-sufficient. . . .

If we lose our original self-sufficient mind, we will lose all precepts. When your mind becomes demanding, when you long for something, you will end up violating your own precepts: not to tell lies, not to steal, not to kill, not to be immoral, and so forth. If you keep your original mind, the precepts will keep themselves. (pp. 21–22)

PRECEPTS EMBRACED BY NIGHTINGALE

Moral or ethical conduct was central to Nightingale's view of nursing. Indeed, Nightingale's mission in the army hospitals during the Crimean War was not only to provide for wounded soldiers, but to demonstrate that women could practice nursing, professionally and morally, under the most adverse circumstances. As was mentioned in chapter 1, secular nursing, in mid-19th century England, was not considered an honorable profession. Sidney Herbert, Secretary at War, in his letter asking Nightingale to lead a nursing expedition to the Crimea, wrote that this project would not only help the soldiers who were risking their lives and thus "deserving everything at our hands," but would also change a long-standing prejudice against professional nursing:

> If this succeeds, an enormous amount of good will be done now, and to persons deserving everything at our hands; and a prejudice will have been broken through, and a precedent established, which will multiply the good to all time. (dated Oct.15, 1854 and quoted in Cook, 1913, vol. 1, p. 153)

Nightingale's standards for nursing practice were incorporated into the curriculum at the Nightingale Training School at St. Thomas' Hospital, which was founded in1860. Students were evaluated monthly on "personal and moral character" as well as on the technical elements of patient care. Items on the evaluation form included personal neatness and cleanliness, sobriety, truthfulness, punctuality (especially as to the administration of food, wine, and medicine), quietness, trustworthiness, and honesty (especially as to taking petty bribes from patients) (Baly, 1986).

Although she put emphasis on rules of good conduct, Nightingale also expressed sentiments similar to those of Zen Master Roshi

Suzuki. She explained in *Suggestions for Thought* (1860/1994) that as we evolve towards full wholeness as human beings, that is, as we become fully integrated with the inner God-consciousness, our behavior becomes spontaneously good:

> The more our state of being is human, manly, in the proper sense of those words, the greater will be our repugnance to what is morally wrong, till willfully to do wrong shall become an impossibility. The mind will *accord* with what is right, which is God's thought or consciousness, or will thirst and long and strive to do so, not in fear of His anger, but in love of right—of God, the living consciousness of right. (p. 95)

The Precepts in *Notes on Nursing*

In Nightingale's view, nursing is a spiritual process. Her thoughts are consistent with those of nursing ethicists Bishop and Scudder (1996) who hold that nursing is an intrinsically moral process because its concern is the well-being of others. Indeed, if we follow the principles of nursing care described in *Notes on Nursing* (1860/1969), we find that we are spontaneously keeping the moral precepts of the great religions. For example, as nursing facilitates healing, that is, the inner tendency towards wholeness, violence or any kind of disruptive behavior is antithetical to it. Nursing is based on compassion, which involves respect for the patient's integrity, so stealing and sexual misconduct are also inconsistent with the process of nursing.

The abstention from lying is a precept that Nightingale discussed at length in *Notes on Nursing* (1860/1969). She believed what all the great spiritual traditions teach: that the divine reality is the essence of truth. Thus the more attuned we are to the inner divine nature, the more our behavior partakes of its truthfulness. And this truthful manner brings great relief to the sick:

> I would appeal most seriously to all friends, visitors, and attendants of the sick to leave off this practice of attempting to "cheer" the sick by making light of their danger and by exaggerating their probabilities of recovery. . . .
> The fact is, that the patient is not "cheered" at all by these well-

meaning, most tiresome friends. On the contrary, he is depressed and wearied. . . .

He feels what a convenience it would be, if there were any single person to whom he could speak simply and openly, without pulling the string upon himself of this shower-bath of silly hopes and encouragements; to whom he could express his wishes and directions without that person persisting in saying, "I hope that it will please God yet to give you twenty years," or "you have a long life of activity before you." (pp. 96–8)

For Nightingale, honesty was not only essential in direct patient care, but also in nursing administration and education. She challenged the traditional religious teachings about cultivating humility and checking pride, writing that these two extremes should be transcended by an honest evaluation of one's abilities. "What I want is a true estimate of myself, not a false one," she wrote. "I want to see myself as God sees me." As one of the greatest nursing administrators, she believed that both *higher* and *lower* positions ought to be used for growth:

Everybody ought to command. No one's faculties are fully called out till they do command. There is nothing so invigorating, so inspiring, so regenerating. Everyone ought to obey. How delightful it is to obey some one who really knows what he is about, and can teach you— to learn, when one really feels that one is learning something. (*Suggestions for Thought,* 1860/1994, p. 133)

For Nightingale, nursing was serving God by serving humanity, whose inner essence is divine. Therefore, the aggrandizement of the personal self, particularly at the expense of the patient's welfare, was, to her, antithetical to nursing. For example, in her discussion of 24-hour management, Nightingale wrote that we must give up the idea of being physically indispensable, however important that makes us feel, and organize care so that a patient's needs are filled as much in our absence as in our presence. This principle applies not only to direct patient care but also to the administration of hospitals and other facilities (*Notes on Nursing,* 1860/1969).

Conduct Guided by Natural Law

Nightingale's view of moral conduct in nursing went far beyond the keeping of religious precepts. From her perspective, nursing is an act of cooperation with nature, which is regulated by universal laws or "thoughts of God." Thus proper conduct will always be determined by our knowledge of the laws, or organizing principles, that underlie the healing process. For example, when we understand the critical relationship between sanitation and health, a minor act such as opening a window takes on a new significance. As Nightingale wrote, it becomes "a religious act to clean out a gutter and to prevent cholera" (Quinn & Prest, 1987, p. 18). Again, when we understand the relationship between energy conservation and healing, it becomes a religious act to provide patients with warmth and quiet. And when we understand the relationship between stress and healing, it becomes a religious act to calm ourselves before entering a patient's room.

In the following passage from *Notes on Nursing* (1860/1969), Nightingale discusses a similarity between good conduct and official politeness:

> Always sit within a patient's view, so that when you speak to him he has not painfully to turn his head round in order to look at you. Everybody involuntarily looks at the person speaking. If you make this act a wearisome one on the part of the patient, you are doing him harm. . . .
>
> This brings us to another caution. Never speak to an invalid from behind, nor from the door, nor from any distance from him, nor when he is doing anything.
>
> The official politeness of servants in these things is so grateful to invalids, that many prefer, without knowing why, having none but servants about them. (p. 49)

If a nurse is careful to sit within a patient's view so as not to create undue exertion or discomfort, he or she is knowledgeably abiding by the law, or relationship, between energy conservation and healing. The gesture might look the same as official politeness, but it is meaningful on the part of the nurse and could never degenerate into an empty formality.

Also, when people are ill their self-esteem is often lower than usual, and thus respect becomes important element of care. This could be another reason that Nightingale found the ill to be so grateful for the "official politeness of servants."

In Nightingale's view, the divine laws of nature are the true "commandments of God." And as our understanding of these laws increases and deepens, our behavior will change accordingly. Good or moral conduct is, thus, not a fixed set of rules, but modes of behavior that are continually evolving.

REFERENCES

Baly, M. (1986). *Florence Nightingale and the nursing legacy.* London: Croom Helm.

Bishop, A., & Scudder, J. (1996). *Nursing ethics: Therapeutic caring presence.* Boston: Jones and Bartlett.

Calabria, M., & Macrae, J. (Eds.) (1994). *Suggestions for thought by Florence Nightingale: Selections and commentaries.* Philadelphia: University of Pennsylvania Press.

Cleary, T. (Trans.). (1995). *Dhammapada: Sayings of Buddha.* New York: Bantam Books.

Cook, E. (1913). *The life of Florence Nightingale* (2 vols.). New York Macmillan.

Gerardi, R. (1989). Western spirituality and health care. In V. Carson (Ed.), *Spiritual dimensions of nursing practice.* Philadelphia: W.B. Saunders.

Goldie, S. (1983). *A Calendar of the letters of Florence Nightingale.* Oxford: Oxford Microform Publications.

Knox, M. (Trans.). (1956). *The Holy Bible.* New York: Sheed and Ward, Inc.

Maurice, F. D. (1957 reprint). *Theological Essays.* New York: Harper.

Nightingale, F. (1959). *Notes on nursing; What it is and what it is not.* New York: Dover Publications. (Original work published in 1860)

Pagels, E. (1979). *The Gnostic gospels.* New York: Vintage Books.

Quinn, E., & Prest, J. (Eds.) (1987). *Dear Miss Nightingale: A selection of*

Benjamin Jowett's letters to Florence Nightingale, 1860–1893. Oxford: Clarendon Press.

Smith, H. (1991). *The world's religions.* New York: HarperCollins.

Suzuki, S. (1970). *Zen mind, beginner's mind.* New York: Weatherhill

Von Franz, M. L. (1964). The process of individuation. In C. Jung (Ed.), *Man and his symbols.* Garden City, NY: Doubleday.

9

True Work

O ne of Nightingale's strongest criticisms of organized religion is its lack of emphasis on work as a spiritual process.
In *Suggestions for Thought* (1860/1994) she indicated that
all occupations could bring us to God, if only we knew how to
perform them in an appropriate manner:

> None of the great reformers have ever taken the way of life into account.
> Wesley [the founder of Methodism]—how much in earnest he was!—he
> preached and people were glad to hear. But did he say to the people, "Now
> while you are washing can you be in accordance with God?"
> There must be washing, and ironing, and building, the earth must
> be cultivated; we must have food, and drink, and shelter. How can
> these occupations be organized so as to be in accordance with God's
> purpose instead of separating us from it? (p. 138)

Nightingale was deeply aware of the spiritual path of action;
indeed, it was a central theme of her spiritual philosophy. "Work
your true work," she wrote in *Suggestions for Thought* (1860/
1994), "and you will find [God's] presence within you" (p. 143). In
this chapter, we will explore Nightingale's understanding of work
as a spiritual process, what makes work *true* or *untrue,* and the
principles which guided her actions.

TRUE WORK IS MORAL

We discussed in chapter 8 that moral conduct, as a dimension of
religion, can help create a resonance between the personal self and

the inner divine spirit, thus strengthening the binding or "connexion between the perfect and the imperfect, the eternal and the temporal, the infinite and the finite, the universal and the individual." From Nightingale's perspective, moral conduct implies much more than keeping religious precepts. It means keeping our work in harmony with the universal laws or organizing principles that underlie health and well-being. For her, the universal laws—revealed through careful observation and statistical analysis—are the true commandments of God. As our knowledge of these laws increases, our idea of morality will become more developed and refined.

For example, Nightingale was deeply concerned about the effects of foul air and water on the health of both humans and animals. She observed them in her clinical practice and also in her statistical studies. In her view, the connections between toxic environmental conditions and ill health are laws, or thoughts of God, and we suffer if we disregard them. "True work," therefore, means dealing with waste products responsibly. Willfully polluting the environment becomes an immoral act, regardless of religious precepts or governmental regulations.

TRUE WORK IS COMPASSIONATE

A compassionate orientation was, for Nightingale, the logical outcome of her spiritual philosophy. If human beings share the same divine nature and are interconnected through universal laws, then working solely for one's own personal benefit is out of harmony with the divine order and thus ultimately self-defeating. It is the evolution of the human race, not specifically chosen individuals, which is the plan designed by a compassionate God. As seen by the following passage, Nightingale had no sympathy with self-centered religiosity:

> Is there anything higher in thinking of one's own salvation than in thinking of one's own dinner? I have always felt that the soldier who gives his life for something which is certainly not himself or his shilling a day—whether he call it his Queen or his Country or his Colours—is higher in scale than the Saints or the Faquirs or the Evangelicals who

(some of them don't) believe that the end of religion is to secure one's own salvation. (quoted in Cook, 1913, vol. 1, p. 488)

Not all of us are given the opportunity to make the ultimate sacrifice for a noble cause. However, there are countless individuals, in all areas of human endeavor, who are working for the greater good. As one novelist wrote, "Not a day passes over the earth but men and women of no note do great deeds, speak great words, and suffer noble sorrows" (Reade, 1861). Reaching beyond oneself creates a resonance with the divine, unitive consciousness and thus, through compassionate work, one can connect with the inner presence of God. And because all human beings are interconnected, the spiritual unfolding of any one individual helps to elevate humanity as a whole. From Nightingale's perspective, it is this effort by so many, largely unrecognized in history books, which has immeasurably furthered the evolutionary process.

TRUE WORK IS SUITED TO ONE'S TEMPERAMENT

Nightingale felt that we should follow our vocation, that is, we should choose work we enjoy and for which we are best suited. Every individual has a purpose, a unique part to play in the evolution of humanity. Thus the greatest gift to God is to follow your inner calling, cultivate your individual talents, and give them generously to the world. Denying your calling, for whatever reason, creates inner conflict and will never lead to happiness.

As we discussed in chapter 1, upper-class British women of the 19th century, like Florence Nightingale, were expected to cater to the family, putting their own talents and interests in the background. In Nightingale's view, this is disrespectfully—and harmfully—throwing away the gifts of God:

> The family uses people, *not* for what they are, nor for what they are intended to be, but for what it wants them for—for its own uses. It thinks of them not as what God has made them, but as the something which *it* has arranged that they shall be. If it wants some one to sit in the drawing-room, *that* someone is to be supplied by the

family, though that member may be destined for science, or for education, or for active superintendence by God, *i.e.*, by the gifts within.

This system dooms some minds to incurable infancy, others to silent misery.

And the family boasts that it has performed its mission well, in as far as it has enabled the individual to say, "I have *no* peculiar work, nothing but what the moment brings me, nothing that I cannot throw up at once at anybody's claim;" in as far, that is, as it has *destroyed* the individual life. And the individual thinks that a great victory has been accomplished, when, at last, she is able to say that she has "no personal desires or plans." What is this but throwing the gifts of God aside as worthless, and substituting for them those of the world? (*Suggestions for Thought*, 1860/1994, p. 99)

Some modern research supports the concept that performing activities one enjoys enhances the integration of body, mind, and spirit. Csikzentmihalyhi (1990; 1975), in his qualitative studies of adult leisure activities (e.g., rock climbing, ice skating, dancing, playing chess, etc.) identified the experience of "flow." Characteristics of the spontaneous flow experience are similar to those of the spiritual practices discussed in this text: one is completely focused in the present moment; the activity is performed for the sake of itself rather than for future rewards; there is a merging of action and awareness, one "becomes" what one is doing; and there is a lack of self-consciousness or a forgetfulness of the personal ego. Of course this is descriptive of play and Nightingale was discussing work, which is supposed to be its opposite. But if one's work is absorbing, meaningful, and freely chosen, then what is the difference between work and play? Could not the two be synthesized?

TRUE WORK HAS A SPIRITUAL INTENT

Nightingale believed that our intent shapes our actions; indeed, it is our motive which makes *any* action either spiritual or worldly. As she wrote in a private note:

It is not the occupation but the spirit which makes the difference. The election of a bishop may be a most secular thing. The election of a representative may be a religious thing. It is not the preluding such an election with public prayer that would make it a religious act. It is religious so far as each man discharges his part as a duty and a solemn responsibility. The question is not whether a thing is done for the State or the Church, but whether it is done with God or without God. (quoted in Cook, 1913, vol. 2, p. 240)

If a vote is cast "with God" then it is not-self-serving; it is cast with the good of the whole in mind. The altruistic intent creates an opening, so to speak, for the divine power to enter and, thus, the action is transformed into a sacred gesture. The transformative power of one's intent was simply and beautifully expressed by Brother Lawrence, a lay Carmelite in 17th-century France, whose spiritual presence affected all who came into contact with him. Some of his letters and conversations are compiled in a volume entitled *The Practice of the Presence of God* (Delaney, 1977). The following are Abbé de Beaufort's reflections on remarks made by Brother Lawrence:

Brother Lawrence spoke to me openly and with great fervor of his way of going to God. . . .

He told me that it consists of renouncing once and for all everything that we know does not lead to God. . . .

That our sanctification depended not upon changing our works, but in doing for God what we ordinarily do for ourselves. That it was a pity to see how many people always mistake the means for the end, attaching great importance to certain works that they do very imperfectly for reasons of human respect.

That he found the best way of reaching God was by doing ordinary tasks, which he was obliged to perform under obedience, entirely for the love of God and not for the human attitude toward them.

That it was a great delusion to think that time set aside for prayer should be different from other times, that we were equally obliged to be united to God by work in the time assigned to work as by prayer during prayer time. . . .

That we should not weary of doing little things for the love of God who looks not at the grandeur of these actions but rather at the love with which they are performed; that we should not be surprised at failing often in the beginning, but that in the end we will acquire a habit which will allow us to perform our acts effortlessly and with great pleasure. (pp. 48–50)

TRUE WORK IS DESIRELESS

Because Nightingale's spirituality was intrinsically active, she was deeply drawn to the concept of *karma yoga*, a central theme in the *Bhagavad Gita* (Arnold, 1975). Indeed, the following passage from this text describes her approach to both spirituality and nursing:

> Do thine allotted task!
> The body's life proceeds not, lacking work.
> There is a task of holiness to do,
> Unlike world-binding toil, which bindeth not
> The faithful soul; such earthly duty do
> Free from desire, and thou shalt well perform
> Thy heavenly purpose. (p. 25)

The underlying theory of *karma yoga* is that the inner divine consciousness can be accessed through "desireless action." It is the ulterior motives and desires of the personal self that bind our consciousness to the earthly realm. If these desires are released, one is free to connect with the spirit. It is important to remember that this concept is not unique to the Hindu tradition. Brother Lawrence, a Westerner, gave us the same message. This is a *universal spiritual teaching* that Nightingale felt should be integrated into nursing practice.

From Nightingale's perspective, the physical world is not meant to remain a "valley of tears." The divine laws that regulate health are open to our exploration, understanding, and application. As she wrote in *Notes on Nursing* (1860/1959), "God lays down certain physical laws. Upon His carrying out such laws depends our responsibility" (p. 25). The evolutionary process, therefore, cannot be fully actualized without human effort. This is our "task of holiness."

In nursing, for example, if we can release our personal expectations and think only of cooperating with the laws of nature, then a greater power can work through us. For the divine reality is revealed not only in the ordered and purposeful processes of nature, but also in the deepest recesses of the human spirit. Therefore, when we align ourselves with the flow of nature, we also align ourselves with the inner divine spirit.

In her personal copy of the *Bhagavad Gita*, the one given to her by Jowett, Nightingale marked the following passage (Cook, 1913), which suggests where her phrase "true work" originated:

> Abstaining from attachment to the work,
> Abstaining from rewardment in the work,
> While yet one doeth it full faithfully,
> Saying, " 'Tis right to do!"—that is "true" act
> And abstinence! Who doeth duties so,
> Unvexed if his work fail, if it succeed
> Unflattered, in his own heart justified,
> Quit of debates and doubts, his is "true" act.
> (book 18, verses 9–10)

Why was this passage significant for Nightingale? Perhaps because it contained a solution for some of her personal difficulties. Like many health professionals today, she worked tirelessly for reform and was often frustrated by inertia, inefficiency, and stupidity within the political system. Sir Edward Cook (1913), her biographer, noted:

> She found it difficult to bear disappointments and vexations with that entire resignation which the mystics taught her. She strove to attain, and she taught others to ensue, passivity in action—to do the utmost in their power, but to leave the results to a Higher Power. (vol. 2, p. 241)

Karma yoga was particularly difficult for Nightingale because she believed in a divine plan of development, in which humanity, as "the working out of God's thought," gradually realizes its spiritual nature and eliminates suffering. Results, therefore, were important. Prevention and treatment of diseases were to improve through the application of scientific principles. But there were many variables, as there are today, and her work did not always bring her the results that she personally desired. The challenge that Nightingale put before herself—and before us—is this: follow your calling, do what you feel to be right, and work for results, but do not become emotionally bound to them.

TRUE WORK IS FOCUSED AND INTEGRATED

It is much easier to be "desireless" when we are focused in our work. We have discussed in previous chapters how unfocused thinking creates tension which impedes our access to the spirit. When we focus ourselves in meditation, relaxation, or prayer, we touch an expansive, timeless dimension of existence. And in the eternal moment, the thought of future results fades into the background. Thus it is the focus, the total giving of oneself, that allows the greatness to emerge from within. In *Suggestions for Thought* (1860/1994) Nightingale wrote compellingly about the need for total concentration in one's work. In the following passage she was responding to the idea, prevalent in her time, that a woman must follow her own interests at "odd moments:"

> The maxim of doing things at "odd moments" is a most dangerous one. Would not a painter spoil his picture by working at it "at odd moments?" If it be a picture worth painting at all, and if he be a man of genius, he must have the whole of his picture in his head every time he touches it, and this requires great concentration, and this concentration cannot be obtained at "odd moments," and if he works without it he will spoil his work. Can we fancy Michael Angelo running up and putting on a touch to his Sistine ceiling at "odd moments"? (pp. 109–110)

Those of us who are not "men of genius" can also do works of greatness. As Brother Lawrence advised, the simplest actions, performed to the best of one's ability and with a spiritual intent, can open the door to the spirit. The story of Prince Wen Hui's cook, cutting up oxen, is a fine example of a mundane act transformed by the creative power of the spirit into a work of art. Here the personal self, totally focused in the moment, becomes an instrument of the *Tao* or *universal spirit of life*. The account, quoted below, can be found in Chuang Tsu's *Inner Chapters* (Feng & English, 1972), a Taoist classic:

> Prince Wen Hui remarked, "How wonderfully you have mastered your art."
> The cook laid down his knife and said, "What your servant really cares for is Tao, which goes beyond mere art. When I first began to cut up oxen, I saw nothing but oxen. After three years of practicing, I no longer saw the ox as a whole. I now work with my spirit, not with my eyes. My senses stop functioning and my spirit takes over. I follow the natural grain, letting the knife find its way through the many hidden openings, taking advantage of what is there, never touching a ligament or tendon, much less a main joint.
> "A good cook changes his knife once a year because he cuts, while a mediocre cook has to change his every month because he hacks. I've had this knife of mine for nineteen years and have cut up thousands of oxen with it, and yet the edge is as if it were fresh from the grindstone. (p. 55)

Why are we not all performing our work as the cook performed his? Because we are not always integrated and focused in our intent. If we apply "ready and correct observation" to ourselves, we have to admit that much of the time we are not "all together." We are doing one thing and thinking of another; we force ourselves to do something we dislike; our intuition says to go in one direction and our intellect says to go in another, so we "wobble" in the middle. Unfortunately, this fragmentation creates friction and energy loss, thus reducing the effectiveness of the action.

A common task, such as sweeping the floor, can serve as a good example. We have all done this in a nonintegrated way, that is, our hands are moving the broom, our thoughts are elsewhere, and our emotions are disengaged from the process. To make sweeping an integrated action, we would keep our minds focused on what we are doing. We would also value the process because it improves, in Nightingale's words, the "health of the house." In this integrated state there is less internal friction, the work flows more enjoyably, efficiently, and creatively.

Integrated action not only improves the quality of our work, it also benefits us physically. For example, Benson's (1996) research revealed that focused exercise can elicit the relaxation response:

> You can also jog and elicit the relaxation response, paying attention to the cadence of your feet on the pavement—"left, right, left, right"— and when other thoughts come into your head, say "Oh, well," and return to "left, right, left, right." (p. 136)

Benson found that by using this approach, joggers achieved in the first mile the "runners high" that usually occurs in the third or fourth mile. He also found that focused exercise is more efficient; that is, less energy is required to do physical work.

INTEGRATED ACTION IN NURSING

Any type of nursing intervention can be performed as integrated action. We have all done it spontaneously in a conducive environment, that is, when there are few distractions and when the procedures are those that we personally find most interesting and/or rewarding. Often, however, the environment is not conducive to integrated work. One of the major frustrations of hospital staff nurses is that their work is constantly being interrupted. In this situation, focused action is not going to happen spontaneously; it will require some conscious planning.

The exercise below includes the principles of both concentrative and insight meditation. Our focus is contained within a certain area and we are mindful of all that occurs within that domain. It includes Chuang Tsu's principle of aligning with the universal life force of the Tao. It also includes Nightingale's intent to cooperate with the organizing principles within nature. From her perspective, nursing is sustained, guided, and ennobled by the universal laws of nature which she called the "thoughts of God."

Start with any simple procedure:

1. Try to minimize potential interruptions; for example, ask a colleague to cover your patients for a few minutes.

2. Take a deep breath, relax, and feel a sense of wholeness within yourself.
3. Make the intent to cooperate with the universal organizing and healing power within nature.
4. Acknowledge the importance of this procedure for the patient's well-being.
5. Keep your mind focused on the process.
6. Be mindful of the patient's responses and your reactions to them.
7. If you get interrupted, try not to become irritated. Acknowledge your emotional response and return as quickly as possible to the work you are doing.
8. When you are finished, let go completely and allow the power of nature to take care of the results.

Don't try to transform all your actions at once, because you will only get discouraged. Start with one procedure, see how it feels, and then *gradually* progress to others. Every day is different, and some days it will be easier to practice in an integrated manner than others. But even *one* integrated action a day will help you replenish your energy and maintain your sense of wholeness.

Some might argue that it is more efficient to do two or three things at once because only then can we be assured that all the work will be completed on time. This might be a satisfactory short-term solution; but in the long run, is it worth the fragmentation, energy loss, and tension that it engenders? It was focused action, totally giving of oneself, that Nightingale felt was essential for patient care. She expressed it simply and beautifully as she concluded *Notes on Nursing* (1860/1969): "Go your way straight to God's work, in simplicity and singleness of heart" (p. 136).

REFERENCES

Arnold, E. (Trans.). (1975). *The song celestial: A poetic version of the Bhagavad Gita.* Wheaton, IL: Quest Books. (Original work published 1885)

Benson, H. (1996). *Timeless healing.* New York: Simon and Schuster.

Calabria, M., & Macrae, J. (Eds.). (1994). *Suggestions for thought by Florence Nightingale: Selections and commentaries.* Philadelphia: University of Pennsylvania Press.

Cook, E. (1913). *The life of Florence Nightingale* (2 vols.). New York: Macmillan.

Csikszentmihalyi, M. (1975). Play and intrinsic rewards. *Journal of Humanistic Psychology, 15,* 41–63.

Csikszentmihalyi, M. (1990). *Flow: The experience of optimal energy.* New York: HarperPerennial.

Delaney, J. (Trans.). (1977). *The practice of the presence of God by Brother Lawrence of the Resurrection.* New York: Doubleday.

Feng, G., & English, J. (Trans.). (1974). *Chuang Tsu: Inner chapters.* New York: Vintage Books.

Nightingale, F. (1959). *Notes on nursing: What it is and what it is not.* Dover Publications. (original work published in 1860)

Reade, C. (1861). *The cloister and the hearth.* New York: Thomas Crowell.

Index

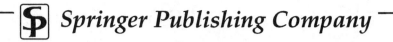
Springer Publishing Company

Integrating Complementary Health Procedures into Practice

Carolyn Chambers Clark, EdD, RN, ARNP, HNC, FAAN

This is a practical guide to integrating complementary/ alternative therapies into a traditional health care practice. It can be used by physicians, nurses, mental health professionals, physical therapists—anyone who wants to augment or enhance their services or simply understand what their patients may be doing on their own to help themselves. The first half provides a rationale and strategies for making a blend of traditional and nontraditional practices work. The second half outlines actual therapies most likely to make a successful complement to traditional practice.

2000   304pp.   0-8261-1288-9   hardcover

536 Broadway, New York, NY 10012 • (212) 431-4370 • Fax: (212) 941-7842
Order Toll-Free: (877) 687-7476 • www.springerpub.com

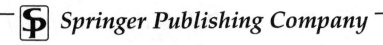

Springer Publishing Company

Wellness Practitioner

Concepts, Theory, Research, Strategies, and Programs, Second Edition

Carolyn Chambers Clark, EdD, RN, ARNP, HNC, FAAN

Now in a second edition, this is a comprehensive resource on health maintenance, disease prevention, and alternative health practices. The author explores conceptual bases and practical techniques for a wide range of programs, activities, and therapies that promote wellness.

Topics include relaxation and stress management, nutrition, exercise, herbal remedies, massage, imagery, affirmations, reflexology, aromatherapy, natural healing, and self-care measures for conditions ranging from hay fever to multiple sclerosis.

Environmental influences and community wellness are each addressed in a separate chapter. Learning exercises are included with each chapter to facilitate integration of the material. A useful resource for nurses, physicians, and other health professionals—both traditional and alternative.

Partial Contents:
- Introduction to Wellness Theory
- Beginning to Move Toward Wellness
- Positive Relationship Building
- Stress Management
- Nutritional Wellness
- Exercise and Movement
- Self-Care, Touch, and Wellness

1996   368 pp   0-8261-5151-5   hardcover

536 Broadway, New York, NY 10012 • (212) 431-4370 • Fax: (212) 941-7842
Order Toll-Free: (877) 687-7476 • www.springerpub.com